SECOND EDITION

MASTERING

COMMUNICATION

AT WORK

HOW TO LEAD, MANAGE, AND INFLUENCE

DR. ETHAN F. BECKER & JON WORTMANN

Mc Graw Hill

New York Chicago San Francisco Athens London Madrid
Mexico City Milan New Delhi Singapore Sydney Toronto

1 2 3 4 5 6 7 8 9   LCR   26 25 24 23 22 21

ISBN   978-1-260-47412-1
MHID   1-260-47412-7

e-ISBN   978-1-260-47413-8
e-MHID   1-260-47413-5

Library of Congress Cataloging-in-Publication Data

Names: Becker, Ethan F., author. | Wortmann, Jon, author.
Title: Mastering communication at work : how to lead, manage, and influence /
  Ethan F. Becker and Jon Wortmann.
Description: Second Edition. | New York City : McGraw Hill, 2021. | Revised
  edition of the authors' Mastering communication at work, c2009. | Includes
  bibliographical references and index.
Identifiers: LCCN 2020043554 (print) | LCCN 2020043555 (ebook) |
  ISBN 9781260474121 (hardback) | ISBN 9781260474138 (ebook)
Subjects: LCSH: Communication in management. | Business communication.
Classification: LCC HD30.3 .B415 2021 (print) | LCC HD30.3 (ebook) |
  DDC 658.4/5—dc23
LC record available at https://lccn.loc.gov/2020043554
LC ebook record available at https://lccn.loc.gov/2020043555

For our moms, dads, and Kelly, Gracie,
Colby, and Abigail, and Jen

CONTENTS

SECTION 1
THE TECHNIQUES

SECTION 2

THE MOMENTS THAT NEED YOUR LEADERSHIP

SECTION 3

A CULTURE OF COMMUNICATION

ACKNOWLEDGMENTS

We are grateful to five decades of coaches and staff at the Speech Improvement Company, Inc., and their hundreds of thousands of clients who through their experiences helped to derive the best practices in communication. To Dr. Dennis Becker and Dr. Paula Borkum Becker for the research and development, and for teaching Ethan plosives at the age of 4. To Kelly, Monica, Greg, and Stefan for their presence and teaching.

To Joe Palmer, Joe Mercedante, Brian Zanghi, Debbie Depp, Carol Long, Jay Therrien, Tim Clark, and James Ebert for your support and insight. To Dr. Robert Wortmann for being the first editor of both editions.

We're grateful to our agent, Giles Anderson, and to our editing and production team: Amy Li, Daina Penikas, Steve Straus, and Alison Shurtz.

INTRODUCTION

A Note on the Second Edition

It's been 10 years since the first edition of this book. It's become an international bestseller, including number one in 13 categories on Amazon. It is read in university classes and sits on the shelves of CEOs of global companies. Leaders and managers use it every day to refresh and to prepare for important conversations and presentations. So what is different in the world that demands a second edition?

Since the first version, information has become a problem. The amount of new data created and shared each day grows so quickly that any stat we could reference is already outdated. The world lives closer together, virtually and economically. While we do not always act as a unified global community, we can communicate instantly, anywhere. Our financial systems, supply chains, corporations, and governments are deeply interdependent. Our methods of communication have changed too. Messaging, virtual collaboration, and live video are ubiquitous. The virtual world is as busy as the real world on a normal day. But is there new wisdom for how we master our communication at work?

In terms of technique, no. Most of what we know about effective communication comes from thousands of years ago when people paid more attention to interpersonal interaction and public presentation. They didn't have media. They didn't have the internet. Aristotle had rhetoric and his voice. His messages still reverberate today.

In terms of people, no. We continue to coach thousands of leaders and managers every year. We all still struggle with the same communication challenges that have plagued organizations and societies of every generation. The formats we taught a decade ago still apply to the same people challenges. Evolution does not move that fast.

In application, however, there are new realities. In this new version, we updated each chapter for the leader who wants to rise in the real and virtual world. We reordered the chapters in the second section. We updated some of the facts and the positional history of our case studies. Unlike some business books, where famous companies that used to demonstrate best practice later failed, the people and organizations we reference continue to thrive.

We also added a new chapter on mastering communication while working from home. We started this chapter on virtual communication long before COVID-19 caused most of the world to work away from the office. The goal of virtual communication is the same as in-person interaction: be clear and be valuable. The way we use language, tone, and timing, however, demands extra care. Words and messages live forever in the digital world. Master communicators love this challenge.

Communication is still the most important skill too many of us take for granted. You are a great communicator most of the time. You have risen, you are rising, because of your natural speaking and listening skills. Do you know how to get better? Do you know the traps that interrupt strong relationships and the measurements that prove you are a leader people trust? We want you to be confident and ready for your people and with your teams all of the time.

Are You Ready?

Are you a leader? Are you prepared to manage? What truly distinguishes leaders from managers is their roles. Leaders have vision, inspire, and provoke others to think creatively. In contrast, managers get things done through others by delegating, measuring results, and holding people accountable.

You recognize the leaders who step onstage, and every eye opens wider. But leaders aren't responsible for what happens next. You know the managers who maintain perfect books and keep you on deadline, yet they couldn't lead you out of a paper bag. One characteristic of both roles is absolutely essential: mastering communication.

Throughout history, master communicators have all used the same techniques and formats. If you don't know what they do as naturally as breathing, you're at risk. You don't need the title of leader or manager to communicate this way. There will be a moment when you are thrust into one of these roles. You have the best idea, and suddenly you are the leader. The leader of your group gives you ownership of a project, and now you have to manage.

Are you ready to be a master communicator who wakes up every morning and knows that you can make a difference?

From presidential elections to every office in any nation, leaders and managers who know how to communicate hold the power. Their ideas are heard, their people love to work with them, and in the end, they tend to achieve whatever they set out to do. They notice the way their people communicate. They adapt their words so that their audience understands the message. They plan what they say, and they know how to listen. They really know how to listen.

The best leaders and managers practice the nuances of how they communicate every day. Clear, impactful communication becomes their instinct. When they deal with the inevitable imperfections of people and organizations, they actually like the moments when most people want to run away. They are the best because they treat communication as seriously as money.

Too many of us think that we can improvise communication, then fail to understand why we don't get the results we expected. Whether with clients or colleagues, one-on-one or in front of a large room, we waste so much time and money recovering from avoidable communication missteps. Master communicators have skills and playbooks to create a culture of communication for the future of their leadership effectiveness and the impact of their teams.

Even if you are the most talented professional in the world, you won't succeed if others don't appreciate your insight. In every industry, conscious practice and measurement of your communication turns ideas into reality and concepts into new worlds. Do you want to be more valuable at work? Are you open to adjusting your way of connecting with people? Can you imagine a world where your communication is a model for your organization? You can be a master communicator.

SECTION 1

THE TECHNIQUES

CHAPTER 1

MATCH YOUR LISTENER'S TENDENCY

Have you ever felt frustrated when someone won't get to the point? Or have you ever felt like the person you're talking to just isn't hearing you? Master communicators navigate these challenges of understanding using an ancient technique that you can learn quickly. This chapter will teach you how to connect with your team.

The First Technique: Match Your Listener's Tendency

How much would you pay to work with the man who studied with Plato for 20 years, expanded every field of human knowledge, and in his spare time coached Alexander the Great (before he conquered the world)? Our understanding of how the best leaders communicate begins with Aristotle. Unfortunately, all we have are his lecture notes. They read like gibberish until you translate his ideas into ways you can communicate differently today. He was the first to recognize that people need information presented in patterns, and that those patterns are distinct. The most important pattern that applies to your work is how you provide the details and make your point.

You'll Know Your Tendency by the End of the First Paragraph

People tend to be either inductive or deductive thinkers. To figure out which someone is, listen for where they make their point. For instance, suppose a coworker says to you that last Sunday he was at a family dinner. His mother-in-law was there, and she said that he should lose some weight. He goes on to say that he found that rude, but based on her comment he decided to take up jogging (stay with us now—this is all on purpose). So he tells you that he went to the mall to get some sneakers. But when he got there, he couldn't find a parking place. So he had to park on the other side of the mall from the shoe store, and when he had walked through the whole mall to get to the store, it didn't have sneakers.

Are you still with him, or do you want him to get to the point? Your answer determines your tendency in the moment.

He keeps talking, and he says that he went to another store, where he found these great white sneakers. He knows his mother-in-law is just going to love them. He's planning to go for a jog this afternoon, and he wants to know if you think it's going to rain.

Inductive Thinkers

Because he is an inductive thinker, he can't just ask if it's going to rain. He is not trying to annoy you or cause you teeth-grinding, fingers-screeching-down-the-blackboard irritation. His brain won't let him ask you about rain if he doesn't first tell you the important details about his mother-in-law and the process of buying his shoes. In his mind, he is being helpful. He believes you need to know all the details first.

QUICK TEST

Does this sound like you? If the coworker in the story sounds like you, you most likely need information delivered inductively (details first). If the story irritated you, you probably tend more toward deductive thinking (details second).

It may sound like babble, but these are not just random thoughts. This is an example of someone who is extremely inductive. He is still inductive if he says, "I just got a new pair of sneakers. I don't want to get them dirty. Do you know if it's going to rain?" The question about rain is the point. Noticing whether it comes first or last is the core competency of mastering the technique. If you are a leader or a manager working with an inductive thinker, you need to communicate the details *before* you make your point if you want your listener to get the message.

Deductive Thinkers

Working with a deductive thinker, your colleague needs the point first. The person still cares about the details of what you have to say, but he will become incredibly impatient if you tell a story or try to ask a question without *first* clarifying what you want.

Take the same example of today's weather. An extremely deductive thinker who does not want to get his new white running shoes dirty and who had the exact same experience with a meddling mother-in-law might simply ask you, "Is it going to rain today?" The most extreme deductive thinkers might not even use a full sentence: They might just say, "Rain?" They want to know about rain, and that is all they'll mention. If your colleague says, "Do you know if it's going to rain today? I just got new sneakers, and I don't want to get them dirty," he is also deductive.

It is easy to feel that deductive thinkers are cold and don't care about the details. You can experience them as curt, even dismissive of the intricacies of what you are trying to say. They do care about the nuances of an idea or story just as much as someone who is inductive. They just need ideas in a different order. If your teammate is deductive, to process the reasons behind what you are saying, he needs the point first. Then he will be able to appreciate the details of your point.

The Recipe

Listeners are either inductive or deductive, and they respond to the kind of communication that matches their natural tendency. Deductive thinkers want the point first and then the details that support it. Inductive thinkers need to hear the details first before they can consider the point.

> Deductive = point first, *details* second
> Inductive = *details* first, point second

Neither way of thinking is better than the other. Matching what your listener needs is most important if you want him to understand you. The first technique is to:

1. Figure out your tendency (whether you are deductive or inductive). It may change in different environments.
2. Determine the tendency of your listener by observing where they put the details.
3. Adjust your communication to match that person's tendency.

The Method

Aristotle did not suggest that one tendency is better than the other. Instead, he realized that different tendencies are more or less effective in different circumstances. If you want to persuade someone with your argument or help him to understand your ideas, you need to figure out his pattern of thinking and match it. When you are in the role of leader or manager, members of your team have to trust you. Matching their tendencies is one way to show that you value them. They will see you making an effort to adjust your communication. *When people know that you value them, they will follow you anywhere and do extraordinary things.*

Why They Drive You Crazy

Here's the challenge and why it is so hard for us. People who are deductive swear that this is the right way to be. The same goes for inductive thinkers. However, the truth is:

Master communicators are able to change the way they communicate so that they meet the needs of the listener. And, most importantly, they are comfortable changing the way they communicate.

Think about that friend or colleague who never stops talking—the one you think is not logical because his points don't seem to connect. If he is inductive, his points do connect—in his mind. Everything he says is extremely important to him. Also, think about that teammate who barely talks because he is extremely deductive. While you value how concise he can be, you also feel that he doesn't give you enough information. *He needs you to start with the point and then follow up with the details.*

If you're the manager and the person who is inductive works for you, not listening to the details first, at least some of the time, hurts the relationship. If you're frustrated, you likely send nonverbal signals that give the impression you don't care about what he has to say. The skill for a master communicator is to stop and give the inductive person your attention.

If you're leading a meeting and the people you're working with are deductive, and you give a long introduction to the initiative you want them to lead, they will stop listening. They will miss what you need from them. The skill is to open with the point—stated concisely. Most meetings need a deductive introduction first so you don't lose deductive listeners. Then, go through the details and finish by restating the meeting's focus. That way you grab both tendencies. The effort is simple, but too many leaders don't pay attention. But why?

It Happens Every Day

It's common for people to feel, "I am who I am, and I don't want to change." This is not about changing who you are as a person; it's about being a stronger communicator. If you are a leader or a manager, *your people will learn from you.* If you practice communicating, they will too. If you build trust with them, they will build trust with their colleagues and clients. The exponential impact on the effectiveness of their work and your organization will be measured not in soft accolades, but in trusted relationships that make success possible. A good leader, regardless of his natural tendency, is fluent in both deductive and inductive communication.

The Colleague Who Pops By

You are the manager. You're sitting in your office, writing an important email to a client or your boss. In comes your chatty subordinate Jerry, who says, "Hi, Bill; did you see that game last night?"

You reply, "Nope."

He says, "Boy, it was amazing," then goes on to talk about it for five minutes, while you barely turn your head toward him and try to hurry the conversation along with a quick "Aha" or "Oh, wow."

Who is inductive and who is deductive?

How does Jerry feel at the end of the conversation, given your short responses? If you had given him five minutes of your attention, how much more comfortable would he feel around you?

Jerry, your inductive employee, doesn't need half an hour. It is normal to worry that he will keep coming by every hour, but after five minutes of real conversation, you can say, "Hey, Jerry, I'm finishing a few things here, but I look forward to our three o' clock meeting," and Jerry will appreciate your listening. When you listen and set the boundary, he is more likely to refocus on his own work. *Even more important, because you have a strong relationship and he trusts you, when you need him to be deductive, he can be.*

Innovation Gets Lost

Your teammate Jeff walks into your office and says, "Sarah, we should spend $50,000 on a trade show."

He read an article about upcoming trade shows. The piece recommended an event in Las Vegas that he feels will make a huge impact on your bottom line for next quarter.

Now, keep in mind that you, as the manager, were in the middle of finishing your presentation for the Board of Directors. All you heard was "$50,000." So, without looking up you say, "Jeff, that's insane."

He walks away from your office, and never mentions the idea again.

Is Jeff inductive or deductive? He immediately got to the point. He is quite deductive and, distracted, you got stuck on the "$50,000." Your response missed his point. What if he had a great idea? Whether you are inductive or deductive, because you were busy you've sent out a message that you don't value his thinking or work. Depending on the severity of your tone, he may think that you don't trust him.

As a manager, when Jeff comes to your office, invest 30 seconds. You will save months of damage control needed to repair the relationship. Stop what you're doing, turn your body to him, and then ask for some background information. Think of it as an investment. You know you have to get back to your presentation, so after a minute or two say, "This is the kind of thinking that I love to hear. I'm going to need more details, and I'm finishing up my Board presentation." Then, set up a time to talk again, or ask him to get this idea on the agenda of a meeting where there's time to explore his proposal further. And if you know you need uninterrupted time to work on your Board presentation, close the door or make sure you protect your creative time.

The Meeting Is Over Before It Starts

Your executive team has to make an essential recommendation to the Board. You have two choices: cut staff or raise capital. You're the CEO. You've asked your chief financial officer to make the presentation and to hold a meeting to get feedback from the executive team first. The CFO is talking casually with the other execs as you show up late.

The CFO opens up with a title slide, then begins by giving a history of the problem for 15 minutes. He then spends half an hour on the analytics and the breakout and 20 minutes talking about the possible directions you could go. Finally, he closes without any action statements and turns it over for questions.

These meetings usually go in one of two ways. The group members may make a few comments about adding a slide or putting a little more text on one of the charts. Generally, they will all say, "Sounds good. See you at the meeting." This is dangerous because the executives weren't listening.

If your CFO gave an inductive presentation like the one we described here, the executives were checking their email, texting, and thinking about what they will do after work. There are inductive executive teams and Boards. Usually not. Most executives are deductive listeners because they have to process so much information and make so many decisions throughout the day. A deductive Board will shut this presentation down in less than 60 seconds, yet your executives didn't because the CFO didn't match their tendency. Their lack of attention set their colleague and the team up for failure.

If you're the CEO and you recognize that the presentation was inductive, the danger is not over because you need to help your CFO come to the conclusion that he needs to be more deductive. What normally happens is bad tact: *you* cut him off in less than a minute, saying, "This isn't ready. Don't you realize we're presenting to the Board tomorrow?" Imagine what this does to your relationship with your CFO and his relationship with the other leaders in the room.

Instead try, "The thing we need to do in the first 60 seconds is show the Board members what we need from them. I know this group. I know they happen to be deductive." Then take the next half hour crafting the message. If your CFO is inductive, he might have a difficult time saying, "We need $500 million." Instead, he'll say, "We need to explore growing operations and perhaps moving our headquarters to Europe"— which is still inductive. Because he is an inductive thinker, your CFO has to talk through the details to get to the point. You need to say, "Try your presentation again, starting with the last slide." It will only feel awkward to the CFO.

When he can say, "Over the next hour, I'm going to share with you why we need $500 million to go to the next level of the business plan," he's ready.

How to Communicate with Rock Stars and the Board: Jon Platt

Jon Platt is one of the most important music publishers in the world. He began his career as a DJ and moved into the business side of music by managing producers. When the professional who bought songs from his clients left EMI, he got the call. As head of its Urban division in the United States, he had a history of signing musicians like Jay-Z, Kanye West, Drake, and Beyoncé.

In 2007, he became president of EMI Publishing West Coast. After EMI, in 2019 he became Chairman and CEO of Sony/ATV, the largest music publishing company in the world, adding artists like Rihanna, Ed Sheeran, and Pharrell Williams.

His challenge is communicating effectively with artists, managers, executives, Boards, and a staff from all over the globe and from completely different worlds. When he began at EMI, a British company, Platt lived and worked in Los Angeles. He had been a giant on the urban scene for years, but was suddenly responsible for all musical genres. To be effective, he had to flow between inductive and deductive communication as easily as he switches from creative development to the executive functions of managing his business.

"I knew the urban field so well that when someone came to me with a question or a comment, within two seconds, I knew how the rest of the conversation was going to go," Platt told us. But that changed when he took over the West Coast catalog, he recalls:

With all genres reporting to me, I had to learn to become a good listener again. Even though it's all music, different genres are run differently. I really had to listen to the whole conversation, or the whole question, or the whole problem, and then try to help the person analyze the best way to get past it. On the other hand, if he's giving me some good news, I need to make sure I heard it.

My style becomes the style of the person I'm meeting with, but I want people to get straight to the point. That's why I had to become a good listener again. If you don't listen, there's always the risk that you think you understand what someone's saying, but you could be on a totally different planet. I can assume you're coming to me with a problem I've handled ten times before, but if I'm deductive, I could be totally wrong. I could totally miss what you need.

Platt changes his tendency based on his listener: "I had to motivate one of my guys, and we had an inductive conversation. I had to go step by step with him: what the job really is, how he was veering off track, and how he could be doing better. Then we had a conversation where we confirmed what we discussed. He never got defensive, and from our conversation, he said, 'I've taken myself out of my shoes and looked at me from a different light, and I look crazy right now.' At that point he wanted to know how he could turn things around. That kept it positive and focused. He was mature and someone who wants to take control of the situation for the better."

Platt is always ready to change his tendency: "I have mentors who were clear that when you have the role of CEO and you have to speak to the Board, the Board members don't want creativity. They want numbers. You have to start with numbers and show how you're making money for them, and then you can back into the creative."

He runs into the same issues when dealing with artists and managers who want him to buy their work:

> The people coming to me looking for a deal are always inductive. I'm a creative guy, but people always send me ten songs. I'll say, "Send me your two best songs." If I want more, I'll ask you for more.
>
> Let's say I'm meeting with a manager who's presenting an artist. He starts with a super glossy bio, but it's all about the music. You spent all this money on this great package, but the music is only halfway decent. You could have put all the effort into the music.
>
> The biggest mistake people make is they don't educate themselves on the person or the company they are meeting with. They do the same meeting for everyone, and that doesn't work.

How Do I Manage One-on-One Conversations?

To listen and speak in the tendency that is not your natural way of thinking is to learn a different psychology. You have to understand a new way of using your mind. Aristotle's recognition of our different tendencies is so profound because it practically involves learning a new language. At first, it seems completely unfamiliar. But when you can translate and engage in the pattern of thinking that reaches your teammates, they will understand what you need and produce better results.

Using the first technique in one-on-one conversations won't be difficult if both of you need the details in the same order. You will probably recognize that strong communication is happening and that you feel comfortable. You still need to pay attention, however, because the other person may switch.

Our tendencies are not rigid. Whether it comes from our family, our education, or our mentors, our propensity to be inductive or deductive is learned. As a conversation changes in topic or intensity, our tendency can change too. People can be deductive listeners and inductive talkers, and the reverse.

The challenge is when the way we process the details doesn't match. You can have a very strong relationship with someone whose natural tendency is the opposite of yours. In that situation, you have to be intentional. As a manager who is having one-on-one conversations in a work environment, when the relationship is not strong and you're trying to make it stronger, you have to pay attention to the natural tendency of your teammates. If you don't, you will create an environment where they won't be comfortable. Worse, they may be afraid to give you critical information.

That doesn't mean that if they are inductive and you are deductive, you have to let them go on forever. Find a place to interject and redirect them to the point. Too many managers who think they are being strong leaders by being direct cut off an inductive teammate and say, "What do you need?" If your relationship is strong enough, you can be that direct.

If you're inductive and you're speaking to someone who is deductive, you may have to practice before the meeting because starting with the point will feel so uncomfortable. In the meeting, try not to think out loud until you get to the point in your thought process. It may feel like others are staring at you. But when you think through what you want to say until you get to the point, then start with the point, the deductive person will immediately feel connected to the conversation and, as a result, to you. To prepare, write down the details and then the point you want to make. Then circle the point, and start the conversation with what you have circled.

If you're deductive and the person you're meeting with is inductive, write down the point you want to make and all the details, then start with the bullets of your outline. If you're deductive and the other person needs you to be inductive, you have to give more background information first. That may be frustrating because you feel that you shouldn't have to, but the other person needs it. If you have read him right and he is an inductive listener, you have saved hours if not days of the person doing the wrong work because he didn't understand what you needed him to do.

If you're not sure of someone's tendency, read his facial expression and body language. You can tell when someone is confused or has shut down. If you see that the other person is frustrated or disengaged, ask him, "Does this make sense?" As you're getting to know him, ask, "Would you like the background info first?" People who are deductive say, "No, just give me the point up front," as if that's the only way to communicate. Those who are inductive say, "Well, of course I need the background first," because to them it is the right way to organize thoughts and present details. The foundation of using Aristotle's discovery about how we think is recognizing that neither tendency is right or wrong. Once you know which way someone likes receiving details, and you deliver information that way, you'll strengthen the relationship.

How Do I Lead a Meeting with Inductive and Deductive Thinkers?

Most meetings include both inductive and deductive thinkers. While executives and Boards of Directors tend to be more deductive, most of us live closer to the middle. You can go to most meetings and not get frustrated unless the person who is talking goes too far in one direction or the other. When someone becomes extremely deductive or inductive, your whole body feels it.

In dealing with mixed groups, decide which part of your presentation should be inductive and which should be deductive. Check your content to make sure it is not extreme toward either tendency because this will always alienate someone. If you are making comments in a meeting, take a reading of the room, and unless you know that the group is definitely leaning toward one tendency, stay close to the center by giving a few details before the point. Then, follow up with a few more details. Don't give all the details first or give the point without any of the details.

When you're talking about things that are new to a group, you can be more inductive because the members of that group need to understand where your point came from. When your topic is familiar, however, you can be more deductive because the background information is already common knowledge. If you can identify the tendencies of the individuals in the group, when you're speaking inductively, look at the inductive communicators. When you're making a deductive argument, look at those who listen deductively. They will appreciate that you noticed their pattern of thinking and engage more.

Consider the behavior of your listeners—their grunts, body language, and eye contact. If it suggests that you have spoken too far one way or the other, pay attention to that and switch. If you're being too inductive, stop talking, continue to think through your process, and don't start talking until you get to the point. If you are being too deductive, think back and give the background information to your point.

All of us get into trouble when we ignore Aristotle. Your Board won't let you. Usually when people are too inductive and the listeners want the bottom line, they will get frustrated or angry, or lose interest. You can see this and match their tendency. You can be in just as much trouble in a weekly meeting with your team members when you like the bottom line and they first want to know, "How did you get there?" They need to know the thoughts that led to your conclusion. If you're paying attention to your relationship with the group, you can contribute in the way its members need to receive information.

PRACTICE THE TECHNIQUE

Drill 1: Discovering Their Tendencies
Usually the frustration is higher when you are the listener.
The key is to simply recognize the tendencies of your team.
At your next meeting:

1. Listen to each person speak.
2. Decide whether she is deductive or inductive.
3. Record your observations.

When we remember that a colleague wants the details in a different order than we do, it minimizes or eliminates frustration because we can change the way we communicate with her.

Drill 2: Mastering the Technique
If you can do this exercise without getting frustrated, you are fluent in both deductive and inductive communication:

1. Think of the most deductive person you know.
2. Have a deductive conversation with her. Write down what you're going to say and how you will say it, putting the point first.
3. See what you notice during the conversation.
4. Do the same thing with an inductive person, putting the details first.

At first, one of these will feel very easy, and the other won't. The conversation doesn't have to be work-related. It could be about your weekend. The key is being intentional about doing it. When you're comfortable communicating in both patterns, if you're in a meeting and a deductive person cuts you off, instead of getting angry, you'll change your tendency. If you're speaking with someone who is going on and on with the details, instead of cutting him off, you'll listen for the point. If you're in a rush, you can let him know that you want to hear the whole story and propose a future time to continue the conversation.

THE TEST
How many times did you get frustrated during conversations today? If you are frustrated, take a note, and later explore whether you were matching the other person's

tendency. Keep track of how many times you get frustrated today, and then do the same thing again in two weeks. Every two weeks keep a record, and you will have specific evidence of the technique's power, or of the work you still need to do.

CHAPTER 2

MANAGE YOUR ETHOS

Aristotle, round two. The Greek term *ethos* translates loosely into English as *ethics*. In communication at work, ethos refers to *credibility*. It is your credibility that enhances your ability to persuade people. Master communicators know their ethos and use it to strengthen the influence of what they say. In this chapter, you will learn what ethos is, how you create it, and why managing it well will help you become a stronger leader and more effective manager.

The Second Technique: Manage Your Ethos

Your credibility determines your ability to lead and manage effectively. Aristotle was entirely correct that communication is the most consistent determinant of ethos. At the same time, you have to manage other qualities that establish what you say is worth listening to.

The Boardroom

The doubt starts when you wake up. You remember that you're supposed to present to the senior executives. You don't need coffee now. You put on what you think they'll like. You have your presentation loaded on your computer, backed up on a thumb drive. You print a hard copy just in case. But in contrast to the racing thoughts as you drive to work, something strange happens as you walk into the corporate headquarters. You feel important! You were chosen to represent your group before the C-suite.

You quickly scan each page to triple-check everything is there. As the elevator door opens, you look up and see the CEO's assistant. Does she know that you're supposed to be here today? You walk down the hall toward two large mahogany doors. You pause and choke down a breath. Entering their world, you see a long wooden table surrounded by leather chairs. Every leader sitting there is a star, at least in your world.

You have to present an hour of material—statistics, metrics, and recommendations. You don't want the executives to be disappointed. You know they have a habit of cutting off people who present poorly. You want them to hear you. You want to be taken seriously. You want to come across as a leader. The question is: Do you have the right ethos?

Perception and Reality

Who has the higher ethos—a Harvard grad or a person who dropped out? What about when we tell you that the dropout is Bill Gates? Your ethos is your credibility. In addition to what you've done and the positions you've held, it's what the people you work with believe you to be, and it changes.

QUICK TEST

What do your colleagues say about you when you're not around?

For instance, in a law firm where everyone else wears suits, the attorney who walks around the office in jeans and sandals may still be the best. His dress and the verve that comes with it add to his ethos as a creative freethinker. But when that same attorney begins to make mistakes, his appearance only increases the perception that he is sloppy and unorthodox.

Your ethos is relative. It changes based on who you are with and the environment you are in. When the CEO of a Fortune 100 company walks down the hall, everyone straightens their posture and politely says, "How are you, sir?" But after shopping trips at home, that same CEO will be asked to carry in the groceries. His ethos at work is commanding and even feared, but when he is with his family, he has the ethos of a well-loved pack mule. In fact, a different ethos at work versus home is why business professionals can struggle transitioning from their work to life at home.

Master communicators are aware of how and when their ethos changes, no matter where they are. The transition from work to home has become complicated as more and more of us work from home. Stress deeply impacts our ability to communicate clearly and effectively. When we become reactive, the part of our brain that seeks to keep us alert and safe causes us to get aggressive, run away, or freeze. With blurred lines between downtime at home and working in the same space, it is easy to lose track of how people perceive us. The ability to change ethos, however, is a good thing.

You can measure your ethos. Aristotle thought that your ethos should be determined solely by how you communicate. He wanted your reputation and your appearance to be irrelevant for your ability to influence people. The old master was an idealist. As certain world leaders and bumbling executives have proven, your ethos is not based solely on how you speak. It is a synthesis of everything that you do and say, your physical appearance, and the reputation of the organizations, people, and places you represent.

You have ethos whether you like it or not. Is it strong or weak? Are you trusted or feared? Do people want to work with you, or would they rather not be on your team? *You first need to know what your ethos is. Then, how you will let others know it.* In some cases, your reputation will precede you and people will learn it from others. If they do not, you will have to invent ways to communicate what makes you credible. As a manager or leader, your ethos will be determined mostly by your behavior.

The Recipe

Every person and every environment is unique. Your ability to adapt will determine the impact of the work you do. Your ethos is what you adapt to create connections:

Ethos = your *credibility*
Your *credibility* = your impact

The second technique for every leader involves:

1. Discerning your ethos with the people and in the environments you want to affect.
2. Figuring out what your ethos needs to be if you are to achieve your goals.
3. Writing a list of behaviors that demonstrate that ethos.
4. Practicing those behaviors until they become natural.

The Method

Begin discerning your ethos by finding trusted advisors to see whether what you feel gives you ethos is both relevant to your position and perceived by others. For example, you may think that your having managed a trade show 10 years ago will help you be a better operations manager today. Will your team see that as credible? You may see the relevance, but others may not. You may think you know your ethos, but until you've tested it with those who understand the people and the place where you work, you may have a dangerous blind spot.

To figure out the ethos you need if you are to reach your goals, ask your trusted advisors to be very specific about the behaviors that mirror the needs of your audience or your environment. You and your team already know people who have succeeded at what you want to do. Do you have the characteristics that they embody? If you went to Harvard, but the people you manage didn't go to college, your Ivy League degree could actually weaken your ethos. You're not going to pretend that you didn't go to Harvard, but you might choose not to emphasize your education as you build relationships.

How will you show others that you have credibility?

The Top 10 Ways to Know Your Ethos

Because your ethos is in everything you do, at first it can seem elusive. How did the leader or manager you want to emulate get so good at what she does? Your ethos is based on your behaviors as well as your accomplishments. To synchronize your ethos, you need to begin by analyzing 10 key areas. This may seem like too many things to think about, but they are not complicated. Any one of them, if you get it wrong, can dampen your success.

In each of these areas, determine the ethos you have and the ethos you need.

1. *Your culture.* Culture has two elements: where you are from and what your organization expects. If you make a mistake in the basic cultural rules of the people with whom you are working, it can have a negative impact on your ethos.

   You were raised in a particular place, and so were your colleagues and your clients. You need to know their way of working and what is considered socially appropriate. Once you know those cultural rules, if you decide that it's important to break them, do so intentionally. Don't let your ignorance lower their respect for you.

2. *How you think.* Whether you are inductive or deductive matters. If the person or group with whom you're speaking needs the details first (inductive), match that tendency. If the people you're speaking to are like most executives (deductive), match that tendency. Matching the way other people think will make it easier for them to receive your message and grow your reputation as a clear thinker and communicator.

3. *How you listen and speak.* Aristotle realized that some people think out loud, while others think internally. Grandma said,

"Think before you talk," but truly, some people can't help thinking out loud. It's their nature. If you notice how much time someone pauses before responding to a question, you can tell whether he is an internal or an external thinker. Measure the silence. Internal thinkers need time to respond to an idea, while external thinkers speak right away.

People can exhibit both tendencies, and they also have a usual way of communicating. As with inductive and deductive patterns of thought, your ethos depends on your matching their tendency. If they need more silence, give it to them. If they love lively conversation with few pauses, listen, but don't hesitate to engage them quickly when they finish speaking. Neither way of speaking is wrong. Matching other people's tendency raises the comfort and positive energy of the conversation. As a result, people will like you more.

4. *Your organization.* The New York Yankees, the Yomiuri Giants from Tokyo, or the Tigres del Licey (Licey Tigers) in the Dominican Republic—which team has the most ethos? It depends on where you are from. All three are famous or infamous, depending on whom you talk to. Ethos is relative, and your organization will either help or harm you, depending on the audience and the environment.

5. *Your title.* CEO is more influential than VP, which trumps director, unless you're in a part of the world where director or managing director is the title of the head of the company. While title matters, your behavior has to live up to the title, and it can be relative depending on the topic. A superstar sales rep may have more ethos than the CEO when it comes to closing a deal, but perhaps not when it comes to strategy. A strong technical support person may have more ethos than the CFO when it comes to fixing computers, but none when it comes to the stock price. So, as you consider title and its impact, consider the context of your audience.

6. *Your past experience.* Stories about what you have accomplished and the environments where you've learned and achieved either positively or negatively affect your ethos. You

build trust when you reveal where you've been successful. Often, a story of past success, with data and how you overcame the hardest problems, is the most powerful way to establish your value.

7. *Your expertise and knowledge.* The areas where you are a specialist, where you have unique insight, raise your ethos. If you keep that knowledge to yourself or walk around bragging, however, your ethos weakens.

8. *Your relationships.* When people trust you, you can borrow their ethos. They will speak highly of you, introduce you to the right people, and support your work.

9. *Your appearance.* Every office in the world has an expected way of dressing. Now, every virtual meeting has an expected appearance too. If you dress too well or too poorly, you will be judged. Maybe you want to stick out. Maybe you want to fit in. The key is to figure out what is effective for the culture. Think about your backgrounds in virtual meetings too. If you appear in front of an epic mountain view in your exquisite home and all your colleagues are in little apartments dodging their children, it will impact your ethos. Pick your style intentionally, knowing that it will affect your credibility.

10. *The results you produce.* When you produce, people have faith in your decisions. When you do what you say you're going to do, people trust you.

The list of factors that create your ethos is not limited to these 10 areas, but if you manage these, there are few relationships that you can't build and few environments that you can't master.

Pictures of Ethos

Ethos Is Relative

A customer walks into a computer store and is approached by two individuals: on the left is the vice president of sales, wearing a suit and tie, and on the right is the tech support engineer, wearing a ripped T-shirt and jeans. Who has the ethos in this situation?

If you said the man in the suit and tie, you could be right. If you said the tech support guy, you could also be right. The answer is: It depends on what the customer needs. If the customer wants 30 computers at a discount, the vice president has greater ethos. If the customer says, "Is this going to work with my printer at home?," the tech support engineer has the ethos. Ethos changes based on the situation.

Ethos Determines What You Can Say and Do

The CEO hands her vice president of marketing an article about a competitor's product. In thick, black letters, she's written diagonally across the front page: *Bullshit!*

There are two possible responses. Either the VP is horrified and goes home to cry, or if the CEO has enough ethos with the VP, this may even motivate him. This may be the kind of honest communication that the two of them will laugh about later and that in the short term expresses urgency to the VP about the importance of the work he is doing.

In this case, the VP laughed about it, knew that the CEO was under stress, and worked harder to get an article about the firm's product published. This is why as a leader or manager you need to care about how you communicate. If your ethos is strong enough, your relationship will be strong enough to absorb just about anything.

Across the Pond

The CEO of an American manufacturing company sat with the CEO of a distribution partner in England for a contract discussion. They were on a conference call with the American company's vice president of operations. After a few polite sentences, the American VP launched into the contract. He talked for over 10 minutes about the contract details, then finished with a description of the penalties if the British company failed to fulfill its obligations.

The American CEO had been watching his British counterpart as he got tenser and more irritated. Too polite to interrupt, the British CEO rolled his eyes when the American VP continued to list the penalties.

Finally, he broke in and said, "If things go wrong, do you think, first, we might just talk?"

The VP made a critical mistake before the conversation. Especially on a conference call, everything is about how many words you use and your tone of voice. He didn't ask his CEO how the other company's executive needed the important information communicated. The British CEO was deductive, and the VP put all the details first. Americans can be perceived around the world as results-oriented bullies rather than savvy long-term partners. By talking too much in a confrontational tone, he only confirmed the stereotype.

How World Champions Communicate: Peter John-Baptiste

In 2007 when the New York Giants won the Super Bowl, a game garnering hundreds of millions of viewers worldwide, what do you remember about the team? If the answer is nothing, that's perfect. The National Football League (NFL) is a business, and its teams function like divisions of a company. When one team has trouble, it is bad for the entire brand. When players behave badly, it can affect the revenue of the entire league. NFL teams want their players to portray a specific ethos. While they want unique personalities, they want those personalities to be focused on football and making a difference in their communities.

At first, new NFL players may not appreciate the ethos they command or their impact on the entire league. These players arrive from college. If you ask many of them why they want to play professional football, they will say, "It has always been my dream." What too many don't realize is that when they go out in public, everything they do affects the NFL, its brand, and its ability to be successful as a business.

Peter John-Baptiste, as vice president of communication for the New York Giants during their Super Bowl runs, managed the ethos for both players and the team. "We took great pride and care in training our players, both on the field in their craft and off the field in their professionalism and communication," he said. "We understand and our players understand that playing in the NFL is a temporary job. We wanted our players to leave with skills that will represent the Giants organization in a positive light. So we helped them learn communication skills and other business management skills. We took the time to mentor new players to behave with a certain level of professionalism."

While these players were celebrities in college, and perhaps nationally if they were the best, there are 700 college football teams and tens of thousands of players. The NFL has 32 franchises and 1,696 active players at a given time. Not all of those make the roster on any given Sunday. New players in the NFL have suddenly entered one of the most elite professions in the world. Everything they do is noticed. If a player behaves badly while out with friends, the public relations department can't kill the story because it appears on social media in 12 minutes from seven different angles. The pain of an NFL player misunderstanding his ethos is that the sponsors no longer want to support the product.

In 2007, two quarterbacks received far more press than Eli Manning: one for running a dog betting ring and the other for drinking with underage women. One went to jail, and the other, a national champion in college, lost his starting job. In 2011, the next time the Giants were world champions, the coaches of another franchise were suspended an entire season for paying bounties to players for injuring specific athletes on the opposing team. Because the players of the Giants paid attention to their ethos both years, all we remember is that they won the Super Bowl.

How Do You Get Ethos?

The good news is that you already have ethos. The question is whether it is helping or hurting your efforts. The three most common ways we gain ethos in business are:

1. It's free (it's given to us, like a title).
2. It's maintained (our performance lives up to expectations).
3. It's earned (our behaviors have taught others that our ethos is strong or weak).

When you meet someone, he has a business card and a title. If what he does and whom he works for carry a high level of credibility, you think of him as having high ethos by association. He didn't do anything, but if he works for a Fortune 500, FTSE 100, or multinational organization, he immediately has a reputation. If his card says CEO, EVP, SVP, or VP; principal, partner, or director; or a professional title like doctor, lawyer, or PhD, you give him ethos.

Just because you get ethos for free doesn't mean that you keep it, however. Ethos also has to be maintained. A company hires a new CEO, and instantly there is excitement. Most likely people were told that he was successful in his last company. But then at the end of the quarter, when the numbers drop, the excitement becomes dread and fear. In the eyes of the employees and investors, the ethos of that CEO drops. If this is you, and you're concerned about managing your own ethos, you need to think strategically about what behaviors you need to implement to change the perception.

If you are just beginning your career or in a new job, you may have to earn your ethos. Again, the focus is behavior. What do you need to do to help everyone around you know that you are valuable, trustworthy, and credible?

You're Young and Ambitious, and You Want to Be a Leader

Gracie is the product marketing manager at a software company, and she has to present to the senior sales team. She's new to the company and was hired for her intelligence and her communication skills. This is her first job in sales and marketing, but the leaders she's presenting to have been in sales for 15 to 20 years. She wants to come across as a strong, confident leader. How does she need to present herself?

First, through careful analysis or with the help of a trusted advisor, she needs to figure out how she is perceived. She is a woman presenting to men. She is younger than all of them, and she tends to dress young. Whether we like it or not, how we look matters. These men happen to be extremely deductive, and they really like a lively debate. If she reads through a preset script, they may feel frustrated and think that she is inexperienced.

She needs to be conscious that in this case, product marketing has a terrible reputation with the sales executives because of poor past performance. It has nothing to do with her, but it impacts her ethos. Last, she needs to know what the sales executives consider important. In this presentation, the only result they want to see is a set of ideas that they believe will let them sell more.

Knowing this, she needs to check off the categories in which she can manage to improve her ethos in the specific amount of time she has to prepare:

☐ Culture	☐ Experience
☑ Details	☐ Expertise
☑ Silence	☑ Connection
☐ Organization	☑ Appearance
☐ Title	☑ Results

In Gracie's case, the fact that she is female, young, and new is a good thing because she brings a different perspective, *but that's not the ethos that will help her.*

Since her title, experience, and expertise don't help, she needs to go and meet with each individual before the presentation. She wants to identify their communication tendencies and build a connection by seeking their insight about what they need from the meeting. She needs to understand the specific areas they want her to focus on and to talk ahead of time about the things they might perceive as negative. She won't be surprised if she prepares. Before the presentation, dressed like a leader in her firm, she can practice delivering her ideas in the pattern that they like to hear.

At the beginning of her time with the executives, she can't claim that she's an expert. She has to borrow ethos from her listeners. She can reference her one-on-one conversations by saying, "I was really glad to meet with you ahead of time to figure out what will be the best use of our time here together." She didn't have to meet with everyone, just with enough key leaders to prove that she's done her homework and that she has buy-in from people at the table for the topics she's about to discuss. After grabbing their attention, knowing they are deductive, she needs to state the point of her presentation first, and offer brief points that support her argument. Then, because they like debate, she must immediately ask questions to spark conversation. The executives will see her as a leader because she built relationships with them ahead of time and because, during the presentation, she communicated in the way *they* needed to feel connected to her and her work.

Bias, Equity, and Ethos

The world has finally begun to seriously consider bias at work. Without realizing it, most of us have preferences. This unconscious favoritism, neuroscience has revealed, is natural. We like people like us because it seems to keep us safe. In the evolution of human beings, it is still biologically risky to surround ourselves with what is different. This impacts ethos in two ways.

First, you may unintentionally be cutting yourself off from the diverse perspectives of your team. If you surround yourself at work with people like you, you miss the different views that create complete decisions and better innovation. The effect on your ethos is that people see you as narrow. They won't view you as someone who has the pulse of the entire organization or a perspective that captures global challenges and solutions.

Second, if you stay in your bias bubble, you'll miss the places where, as a leader, you can promote equity. The future of organizations is inclusivity of hiring, team building, and culture. Inclusive teams are smarter. As the global economy grows, leaders whose teams can appreciate the breadth and complexity of problems and opportunities will be the most successful. Implicit bias keeps you from seeing the people, the partners, and the organization you need to win. Losing, it turns out, isn't good for your ethos.

How to Be the First Female Leader of the Central Bank of Malaysia: Dr. Zeti Akhtar Aziz

Malaysia has always been a magnet for investors. Its economy rapidly recovered from the Asian economic crisis in the late 1990s, and it has enhanced the resilience and stability of its financial system. To date, there have been nine governors in the 50 years of the Central Bank of Malaysia's history. Dr. Zeti Akhtar Aziz, who served by appointment of the king and prime minister, became the central bank's governor in 2000 and served as its first female leader until 2016.

The central bank's responsibilities—issuing currency, promoting monetary and financial stability, and driving the development of the financial system—made Zeti's communication critical to the ethos of Malaysia in two ways: first, as a public speaker and second, with her team. As a speaker, she was continuously sought after to deliver keynote speeches in the financial industry around the world. Zeti told us: "As the Central Bank, we are responsible for the economic and financial conditions of the country. We therefore touch the lives of every individual because everyone deals with the monetary and financial system. Whenever there is a financial crisis, the Central Bank will be at the forefront to restore stability and recovery." She has a powerful, calm, and wise speaking style that inspires. As the governor, one wrong word can destabilize and send the financial system into chaos.

Her communication internally was just as sensitive. "I was the acting Governor in the late 1990s during the height of the financial crisis in Asia," she said. "When the Governor resigned, the Prime Minister called me and asked me to be the leader. He told me the two reasons why he selected me. One was that I knew how the system worked, and the second was that I stood in high regard with the people." The Prime Minister knew that there had been a problem with the ethos of the Central Bank, and bringing on board someone who was deeply respected was the first step in changing that ethos:

It was a defining moment for the Central Bank and for the country. A number of currencies in the region had collapsed. There were several waves of severe speculative pressure, and it was my opinion that a few more rounds of such speculative attacks would have brought our currency to meaningless levels. Such an outcome would have resulted in total devastation of our economy. During this time, I had already been part of a team that had begun restructuring the financial institutions to get them to resume lending. A credit crunch had to be avoided. If the ethos of the Central Bank is in question, the financial institutions would not have the confidence to lend the money needed for companies to survive and grow, which would in turn have a spiral down impact on the overall economy.

Back then, the tension ran high, but the feeling within the Central Bank was of great determination not to let the country down. To keep people motivated and focused on achieving the right outcome, I communicated that failure would not only result in high costs to the economy, but also cause total devastation. I communicated with the team every day.

In this case, to get an entire organization to change its ethos, the program needs to be seen as a change effort, which means identifying a catalyst for change. Without a catalyst for change, it is virtually impossible to change the ethos of an organization past a new logo, letterhead, or tagline.

The drive toward avoiding total economic devastation, you might say, is an effective catalyst. When you get your internal leaders on board, that change will penetrate the entire organization in a positive way. That will change your ethos in the eyes of the public. For example, Zeti recalled:

When we implemented capital controls after more than one year into the crisis, we were totally condemned by the entire world. The international agencies and fund managers were angry. To accomplish our goal, I communicated to our leaders that we had to do only those measures that would achieve our objective, instead of the wide-ranging measures that were being proposed. The ability to articulate our positioning on the proposal was key in convincing the leadership on the manner in moving forward with the proposals.

My team worked day and night to implement the measures. The importance of confidentiality had to be reinforced until we were ready to go public. The risk was too great. We had to be successful.

In this change effort, the planning was only known within the organization until the communication was ready to be rolled out. If word of the proposed actions had leaked out, it would have fueled the fire of the skeptics and perhaps undermined the effort.

When you are planning to roll out an ethos change, you've got to know what the new ethos is, how you will implement it, and what behavior changes you will make to demonstrate that ethos. It's not enough to just talk about it. You need to have everyone on board, you need new policy or behavior that will support the new ethos, and you need your leadership in the public eye championing the changes. As a result of Governor Zeti and her team's hard work, Malaysia has changed its ethos from having a currency in the region that almost collapsed to having a prompt and stable economic recovery. The economy has since continued to grow through the peaks and troughs of a more challenging global environment.

PRACTICE THE TECHNIQUE

Drill 1: Discerning Your Ethos

You need feedback to figure out what people think of you.

1. Get feedback from a qualified teammate on the 10 key areas listed earlier in this chapter.
2. Take a personality profile like Myers-Briggs, DISC, or CANOE—the profile favored by psychologists today.
3. Record or videotape yourself during a one-on-one conversation, meeting, or presentation.

The person who helps you discern your ethos needs to be someone you can trust—meaning that she doesn't have any agenda other than your success—and she has to be qualified to help you. If she doesn't have the intelligence, background, and experience, or if she doesn't have the right ethos, her judgment won't reveal who you are at work. Find someone who is qualified—a manager, mentor, communication advisor, or even someone who works for you whom you trust not to lie to make you feel good—and ask her to describe you based on the 10 key areas.

Personality tests may reveal your preferences and how others will see you. They tell you what you are so that you can use the techniques to communicate in such a way that colleagues and clients experience you as a leader. The weakness of these profiles is that too many consultants and professionals present their results as being unequivocally who you are. No test can permanently label you. These tests are a measurement of your preferences today, and if you choose, you can change your behavior so that you are seen differently.

Having a recording of what you sound like when you are communicating in your present role will reveal volumes about your ethos in that setting. If the people you are working with are uncomfortable being recorded, say, "I'm working on my communication. I want to record our conversation as a learning tool so that I can improve." Your honesty and desire to work on your communication may improve your ethos with them. If not, find another group to support your development.

Drill 2: Changing Your Ethos
There are people who are already masters of the ethos you want to project.

1. Pick three leaders who exhibit the ethos that you want to have.
2. List the characteristics and behaviors of each leader that create the ethos you want.
3. Cross-list those characteristics and behaviors that are the same for all three leaders, and practice them.

The reason to analyze three leaders is to contrast their behaviors. As you process your observations, it will expose the behaviors consistent with the ethos you want to develop. If all three leaders are doing something, that behavior will certainly be effective for you.

THE TEST

Did you get the reaction you expected? At your next meeting, note the reaction of your listeners. First, look at their body language and eye contact. If your ethos is high, they are listening attentively, taking notes, and waiting for your next word. Or, if you're in a communication culture that emphasizes dialogue, your teammates speak without fear, debate ideas enthusiastically, and want to know what you think.

Second, when they respond to your questions or ask their own, notice their tone. If you have the ethos of an effective leader and manager, they will be respectful. They won't necessarily be deferential—this depends on your culture—but they won't be dismissive. They may challenge your ideas—challenge can be the best validation that you have a high ethos—but they will not be condescending.

CHAPTER 3

SPEAK TO MOTIVATE

Speaking to motivate maximizes employee engagement. Not everyone is motivated by the same things, and the same person might even be motivated differently based on the topic. In this chapter, you'll learn a technique—the motivation matrix—that will help you figure out what motivates different people and how to choose your language and tone so that you can motivate almost anyone.

The Third Technique: Speak to Motivate

People may do what you want because you are the boss, but you may not necessarily get their best work. Almost everyone wants to give their best. Almost. There are some teammates, no matter how hard you try, who just won't care. They do things for themselves. Why? Mental health, past trauma, family or cultural background, personality differences, or the job is simply not a good fit. There are reasons you will struggle to connect with some people. The occasional relationship that flames out can be reason to connect more deeply with the rest of your team. Discover what drives your team. If you do, they will take ownership of their projects and, most days, love what they're doing.

QUICK TEST

Of the people you lead, who is the poorest performer? Do you know what pushes or pulls him to succeed?

The Motivation Matrix

MOTIVATED BY	MOTIVATED FOR		
	Achievement	Recognition (Affection)	Power
Ethos (Credibility)			
Emotion			
Logic			

The Recipe

Every human being is motivated *by* things and *for* things. We are motivated *by* ethos, emotion, or logic. We're motivated *for* achievement, recognition, or power.

By = *push*
For = *pull*

The motivation matrix is simple. You don't have lots of letter and number charts to study. The matrix is based on figuring out both push and pull so that you can craft your language about your expectations in ways that engage people's natural desire to perform. As you think about the people you hope to motivate, the third technique for every leader is to understand:

1. What are they motivated *by*? What pushes them? If they're motivated by ethos, the question is, which authority asked for the work to be done? If they're motivated by emotion, it's, is the project exciting, dangerous, or urgent? Or if they're motivated by logic, it's, is this the practical, reasonable, right thing to do?
2. What are they motivated *for*? What pulls them? If they are looking for achievement, they want an honest day's pay for an honest day's work. If they're looking for recognition, they want pats on the back in front of the team. Or if they want power, they want authority, control, and the ability to make decisions.
3. Speak to their motivation by crafting language that pushes and pulls their drivers, not yours.

Where people fall on this matrix is dynamic. It may be different at work and at home. It will be different for the different members of your team. People may even fall in different places based on the topic. As a leader or manager, it is essential that you have a solid sense of where your people are coming from. If you don't know, that's your homework.

You learn from listening to their stories. For instance, at lunch a customer service manager told you that she started running a general store out of her bedroom when she was eight. She sold goods to her stuffed animals, excellent customers like Brown Bunny and Jerry the Giraffe, through her store manager, Teddy Oregano. To ensure that her customers were happy, she offered a discount for return customers. From this story, you can immediately learn what motivates your teammate. She's motivated by logic (exhibited by giving discounts to bring back customers), and for power (she's been running businesses since she was eight).

If you can't comfortably place your teammates on the motivation matrix, that exposes a key area in your relationship that needs time and energy. Why do they do this job? Why are they staying in your organization? Knowing these kinds of details allows you to talk about what needs to be done in a way that will get them excited about doing the work.

The Method

Too many managers pick one approach to motivating their team and stick with it. They default to the way they want to be pushed or pulled and assume that everyone is like them. Or they use what has worked in the past without taking into account their present environment and how it is unique. Adapting your approach for each person can feel artificial at first, and it may seem like it will take too much time. How much time do you spend engaging teammates who don't connect to the challenges your organization faces today? If you could have one clear conversation with each member of your team and know that she was excited, truly excited, about completing her projects, how much time would you save? How much more effective would she be?

Can you place your people on this matrix? The motivation matrix is a tool to guide you. As people can have different motivations in different contexts, now you can adapt. There are very few leaders who can immediately speak to motivate off the top of their head. Over time, it gets easier because you recognize your teammates' drivers and what they need.

The Specific Words

Imagine that you need to complete a project in two weeks, a month ahead of schedule, to meet your customer's new deadline. Your CEO, Gordon, has asked you, his vice president of operations, to make sure that it happens. You have strong ethos with your team, but not as good as the CEO's. Here's what you say, depending on your team members' motivations.

MOTIVATED BY	MOTIVATED FOR		
	Achievement	Recognition (Affection)	Power
Ethos (Credibility)	Gordon needs this done in two weeks.	We created a new bonus program. Gordon will present the awards at the company meeting if we meet the new deadline.	Gordon wants you to run the group if this project comes in on time.
Emotion	I know we can get this done on time, and I know you're the person for the job!	We created a new bonus program for top performers. We'll give out the bonuses at the company meeting if we meet the new deadline!	The group is yours if we get this done on time!
Logic	They gave us a new deadline, and when we get it done, I'll get you comp time.	They gave us a new deadline, so we've created a bonus program for those who help us meet it. Awards will be presented at the company meeting.	They gave us a new deadline, so whoever contributes the most hours will get to run the next project.

What Pushes People to Succeed?

What people are motivated *by* is what impels them to produce. It is the part of their relationship to the people and environment where they work that *pushes* them into getting projects done. Again, the three categories are ethos, emotion, and logic.

Ethos

If you are motivated by ethos, you feel moved to work harder because the person who asks you to do the work has credibility in your eyes, or when the project is big or important. If your boss doesn't have credibility and you're motivated by ethos, his opinion of what is important may not matter as much. If, on the other hand, he says that the CEO wants you to do this project, that it's the one that everyone else wants to work on, you jump. For others, credibility does nothing. If a celebrity tries to get through airport security and the guard is not motivated by credibility, the famous person waits. But if the governor shows up at your restaurant, you're the host, and ethos matters, you give her the best table.

Emotion

Someone who is motivated by emotion gets fired up easily. When you come to such a person and say, "Can you believe what Tom just said?" He replies, "Oh, really? *Nooo*, I can't believe it." This person responds when you say that you need something done right away and it's urgent. In fact, it doesn't matter what the emotion is—happy, sad, or angry. This person needs to see emotion to care about what he is doing. Again, this doesn't work if the person is pushed by ethos: he will look at you and scoff, "You can't tell me what to do." The logical person will say, "Stop your whining." For the person who is pushed by emotion, seeing your emotion gets him motivated.

Logic

Someone who is motivated by logic needs to understand the reasoning behind what she is doing, and she needs to hear it from you in a logical way. She needs you to speak in a calm, clear tone that reveals why what needs to be done is important, what thought brought you to this point, and how that will be the best solution. For instance, an IT team is setting up for a conference, and it's taking longer than planned. If the team members are motivated by logic, and the manager says, "The CEO wants this done," they won't care. If he says, "We *have* to get this done!" they will tell him to relax. But if the manager says, "Two of the computers aren't working. Looks like it's a software problem. We need them at 9 a.m. So we're going to skip the opening reception and we'll get dinner when we're finished." They will finish without thinking twice.

What Pulls People into a Project?

What people are motivated *for* is what they are motivated toward. It is the part of their relationship to the people and environment where they work that *pulls* them into action. The three categories are achievement, recognition, and power.

Achievement

If you're motivated for achievement, and your job is to prepare the annual report, you just want to get it done. You don't want a mention at the annual meeting or your name on the cover, and you don't want to hear that if you do a good job, you can run the project next year. This type of person rarely needs kudos and isn't as concerned with his title or career track. People who are motivated by achievement carry their lunch box to work, clock in, and do their job well. They take an hour for lunch. At five o'clock they go home. If you need them to do more, speak in the language they are motivated by (ethos, emotion, or logic) and clarify the job you need them to do. They will get it done because finishing the job to the standards you set is what matters most.

Recognition

Someone who is motivated for recognition needs public acclaim. These people look forward to having their names called at a public meeting. This isn't vanity, and even if you think it is, it is what some of your people need. When they don't get it, they become less motivated. Worse, when you give the recognition to someone else, these people's resentment builds and their productivity starts to drop. Don't give them recognition if they don't deserve it, but make sure you have been clear about what they need to do to be recognized. They want the plaque they can hang on their cubicle wall. But remember, you can't just give a plaque to everyone because people who are motivated for achievement may get offended or not show up for the award ceremony. People who are motivated for power want the award only if it comes with a new title or a project to run.

Power

If your employee is motivated for power, he wants control. He needs the ability to make decisions and the authority to direct the outcomes of his projects. When a power-motivated employee doesn't have control, he can be passive-aggressive and not collaborate. When he feels completely unmotivated, he can sabotage others' work in order to feel that he is in control. Instead of telling a power-motivated person what to do, ask questions so that he can come to the decision on his own.

While an achievement-focused teammate wants clear expectations and a recognition-focused employee needs public praise, the person who is motivated for power needs the chance to affect his destiny and the future of the company. When you speak to such people about a project, they need to know what they own and how that will give them greater responsibility next time.

Motivation (and Demotivation) Happens in an Instant

The Executive Who Throws Everything off Track

The CEO walks into the meeting and says, "Look at a different kind of marketing with another agency." Because it is the CEO talking, the group, which had run a clear process to choose an agency over months of work, changes all its plans. One comment screws everything up. While the person who is motivated by credibility may be excited about the change and the others may still do it, you have to be careful.

The person who is motivated for recognition just had her ideas shut down, and now she is resentful. The person who needs power will become defensive because control was taken away. Worst, the people at the table who are unhappy may not mention their frustration. They will slow down the project, keeping their best ideas to themselves, because of one phrase. Their energy will drag in the meetings about next steps. This example does not suggest that a leader cannot change direction. You simply have to be strategic about how you communicate the change or your people will lose motivation.

As an executive, you have to know what motivates your team, you have to know your ethos with the group, and you have to plan how you will deliver feedback and suggestions. If you know what motivates the members of your team, socialize your ideas individually and with departments before delivering those ideas to the company. This makes the final message more impactful because they were part of the process. In every case, strategically and intentionally deliver your messages in words that motivate them.

The Damage $100 Can Do

An executive's tech team attends a trade show in Las Vegas every year to evangelize the firm's newest cameras. He thought it would really get the team members going to give the person who got the best reviews from their booth $100 to go gamble. The result: backlash. You'd think everyone would want the chance to earn an extra $100 in Vegas. One member of his team said: "This is our job. You don't have to bribe us to do our job." Motivated by achievement, not recognition or power, they take great pride in their work. The impression that their manager had so little faith in them caused the team to distrust his judgment.

Underpaid and Overworked

You want to motivate your overworked and underpaid employees. That sounds like a joke, but in every business model, there is a ground floor. You have teammates who are interns, volunteers, new, or in jobs that pay very little. You need them. Do you know where they are on the matrix? If not, you can't motivate them.

If you're their direct manager, ask them three questions. Start with, "What do you love to do?" That still sounds like a joke, but it's not. You can't motivate people if you don't know them. Some of the best work experiences can pay little or no money. Because the relationships are so strong, the experience is priceless. This first question gets at what the person likes and gives you clues about his core motivations.

Next ask, "What do you love about your career?" You don't ask him about his job because a job is something that you do for money. A career is something that you invest yourself in and want to do as a center of your life. The person may start talking about an entirely different job, and again, you're learning who he is and what he loves.

Last, ask, "What was the proudest moment of your life?" He may say, "When my son was born." Then you can go deeper with a question like, "What was it about being a parent that made you proud?" Now you will hear words that you can use to talk to him about what he is doing. In each question—and these are only examples of the type of questions that you can use to get to know someone—you reveal that you want to know who the person is. It's about finding what he values so that you can use language that shows that you value him.

Figure It Out with Context

Recognizing that there are specific categories of motivation usually reveals what each employee needs. If you can't figure out where to place someone, however, look at the specific context where you work. Analyze the setting of what you want a person to do. How? Ask them what they want to see happen with a project, for the department, or for the company. Then listen.

Listen to *how they describe the future* and you'll know what they are motivated by, what pushes them:

- *Ethos*. If they talk about the executives, other well-known competitors, and the biggest projects, they are motivated by ethos.
- *Emotion*. Their enthusiasm reveals whether they are motivated by emotion. If the question causes them to get jazzed or troubled, the emotion is a sign that feelings drive them.
- *Logic*. A conversation about the steps the company needs to take and why they are important shows you that the person is motivated by logic.

The same conversation can reveal what they are motivated for, what pulls them:

- *Achievement*. If their comments center around specific tasks, they are motivated for achievement.
- *Recognition*. If they talk about being seen as the best or winning awards, they are motivated for recognition.
- *Power*. If they talk about dominating the competition, wanting to run the group, or running things a particular way, power is the motivator.

They may get quiet when you ask the question. Just wait. Remember that some people think before they speak, and other people think out loud. Neither style is right, and as a leader, you want to make room for people to show you how they think so that you can speak to their motivation. If they aren't willing to say what they think, check your ethos.

It's possible that they don't trust you, and you may have to do that work first. Either way, you've learned what you need to do to build a stronger relationship with your teammates.

People Are Not Only Motivated by Money

Money motivates almost everyone, but for different reasons. For you as a leader or manager, what money means depends on the way you use it. If achievement motivates your teammate, climbing the ladder toward higher compensation means that he has done the job he was supposed to do. Achievement-motivated teammates want to achieve a $100,000 salary because it proves that they have created value. They don't want a party or to have others know. They don't care what title they get. What matters is that they have achieved the salary that is their goal and done the work to earn it. When a manager or CEO is already wealthy, is he motivated by money? Probably not. His motivation is probably achievement—knowing that he has accomplished what he set out to do.

Money can be used to give praise when the recognition is done in public. You can let them know that they have achieved their goal through public recognition in a global email, at the team meeting, or in a quarterly report to the Board. When you give the recognition only in private—at a one-on-one compensation review, for instance—that is actually trying to motivate employees for achievement. Public recognition with money works in a competitive environment where people want to be recognized. It may not be effective around noncompetitive people—like those in an architecture firm or some consulting practices—where collaboration is the goal.

For most people, money does mean power. The more money you have, the more things you can do. Money means that you can control whether you buy a new car or a home. In the global business world, the more money you make, the higher the value you have. With more money, you have more authority. But it's not an absolute. Some people think that the more money you have, the shallower you are. You might expect that a CEO makes the most in a company, but in many organizations certain VPs have negotiated better deals. Money is rarely the only end goal. Use it to speak to *your employees'* motivation.

Not Everyone Is Competitive

Your most talented people, the ones who have helped you get your big wins, may not be competitive. If this makes sense to you, skip this paragraph. If not, chew on it for a second. They may not be like you. You want to be the best, and so do they. But they don't want to battle. They absolutely are motivated to get the job done, and depending on what they are motivated for, they want to either simply get it done and go home (achievement), get it done and be praised for it (recognition), or get it done so that they can run the next project (power). For them, however, work is not a sport.

Too many leaders assume that everyone is competitive. The person who has never played sports in his life may not appreciate what you mean at meetings when you talk about "knocking it out of the park" or "being a team player." You mean excellence and collaboration, but your choice of metaphors irritates them. Suddenly, they are demotivated. If you see things through the filter of winning or losing, and they don't, eventually they will leave. Use the language of business and organizational behavior instead of sports. People who are not competitive are just as capable of helping you reach your goals. Speaking their language proves that you are a leader they can trust.

How to Motivate 1, 10, or 10,000 People

The difference is precision. When you speak to a smaller number of people, you can be more exact about speaking to the particular drivers that excite your colleagues or your team. Mechanically, there is no difference in *the final step* between motivating in a one-on-one meeting with an employee and delivering a webinar to a company of 100,000. In any environment where you want to motivate as a leader, in planning what you say, you have to match your tone to the substance of what you're communicating.

For example, if you are introducing someone at a meeting, virtual or live, and you respect her, your voice has to show it. If you are monotone or flat, it steals the ethos of the person you want the audience to appreciate. If your presentation or conversation is emotional, you have to put feeling into your voice. The politicians who can't match their tone to the gravity of the moment aren't trusted, or they simply lose the election. When you're speaking about a very logical topic, your voice and tone should sound logical or your ethos goes down.

If your tone matches your topic, you sound authentic. For instance, if you're talking about last year's revenue using numbers and graphs, that seems like a logical presentation. But is it? What do those numbers mean? You just told your team that you doubled your profit over last year's. That's a huge deal. However, when you don't sound like it's a big deal, you become a bit less believable. Or, at least, less interesting. For a leader, this doesn't motivate your team.

When your tone and your topic do match, it's motivational—even when it's negative. Your team members want you to show them the important work that has to be done. Negative results can provide purpose. If you're presenting the logic, you have to have a steady, reasoned tone. When you are inspiring people to take the next steps, your voice has to convey your excitement. No matter how many people you talk to, if you present a mixed message, they will retain only part of the information and be unclear about which parts you want to emphasize. It's not enough to simply have great content. If you want to motivate people, match your tone of voice with the content.

How to Motivate Cross-Culturally: Andrew Brien

Andrew Brien and his executive team manage 200 employees. They changed their culture from one of fear to one of collaboration. Teammates would talk about each other, but not to each other. Management wasn't hearing about negative news, and managers found out about problems only after the fact.

Brien is CEO and Executive Director of Suria KLCC, a billion-dollar shopping complex at the base of the Petronas Towers in Kuala Lumpur. As the global financial crisis hit in the fall of 2008, commercial real estate firms began laying off their teams and filing for bankruptcy. Suria KLCC didn't lay off anyone. One of the methods it uses to drive performance: Pay attention to the distractions that take people away from their daily work.

Brien is from Australia, and most of his direct reports are from Southeast Asia. At home, a more direct style was usually effective. When someone was not performing, Brien simply told the person what he thought. From the deductive and direct communication, the employee took that feedback and improved. When Brien first joined Suria KLCC, he used that approach, and it hurt his relationships with his teammates.

"You have to ensure that people do not feel bad about what you are saying, are not put on the spot when they don't perform, or are not seen by others as not performing," he says. "While you need to do those things sometimes, there are other times where they're just not going to work." He had to overcome the issue of "face," which translates as a person's honor. You can't motivate someone who works for public recognition by criticizing him in front of others.

Brien notes that "From my dealings in Asia over the last five years, face issues can often be helped by taking a bit of pace out of the deal or negotiation or relationship, by getting to know someone a bit more personally. That way you can identify whether he is an ethos, emotion, or logic person. You can work that out through the social aspects of getting to know him."

Speaking to motivate starts when you understand the other person's perspective, says Brien: "If you can show some empathy, people will open up to you more. Particularly in an Asian environment, you get less of the 'yes means no.' You don't have to talk about everything, just about little snippets of things that might not even be in the current job. It could be something from five years ago, something you've learned that is applicable today in the situation they're in."

An essential in motivating is the ability to be vulnerable. Brien suggests: "Talk about the times you've screwed up. Everyone does it. Unfortunately, there are a lot of leadership books that have been perfectly written by the perfect leader. Very few of them say, 'I really screwed that one up.' To connect with people, admit that you've been wrong."

And when you admit that you don't always get it right, you can be more intentional about looking for what is right for others. Motivating employees is even affected by where you have the meeting. For example, says Brien: "If you have a team member who is unsure of her destiny, or of whether she wants to be here, and you want to keep her, the worst thing you can do is hold that meeting in your office. You need to build the emotional part of the relationship with that person. We've been talking with a particular person for several weeks, and all those conversations have happened outside the office for that very reason." Sometimes the ethos of you in your office is so strong that it can prevent a connection.

For Brien, techniques that build trusting relationships, like speaking to motivate, are an economic decision: "Let's face it, organizations don't have a churn rate because they pay low. They have a churn rate because the environment the executives are in is not a healthy environment. If you have good communication, you have a healthy work environment where people feel comfortable and enjoy coming to work, and this pays dividends in your churn rate. It will stop you paying 20 percent to a headhunter every 18 months." In an unhealthy communication environment, employees would leave sooner than 18 months if they could, but they are afraid it will reflect poorly on their career. This leaves you stuck with unmotivated employees on your payroll.

And Brien knows creating a healthy culture of communication isn't easy, so he continues to ask his staff to help him improve: "If we could all have that camera above our desk watching us 24/7, and once a week hit the button that says, 'Highlights of bad communication,' that would be great, but it isn't going to happen. So, I may not be perfect, but I strive to be, and I appreciate it when my staff lets me know when I'm off my game." In order to do that, speak to your staff members' motivation so that your relationship with them is strong enough that they feel comfortable telling you what they need.

PRACTICE THE TECHNIQUE

Drill 1: Knowing Your Team

If you know your team, you can place every single member on the motivation matrix:

1. Copy or draw the matrix.
2. Write the name of each team member in the box that you think fits her most often (remember, this can change in different environments, but most people have a usual tendency).
3. If you have trouble, pick a specific project and context for which you want people to be highly motivated.
4. Plan the language and tone you will use to speak to them the way they need to hear from you.

If you now know what motivates your people, you know what kind of communication you need to practice if you are to build the relationship.

Drill 2: Matching Tone and Message
It's not hard to speak to people's motivation if you remember to match your tone and the substance of what you're saying to motivate them.

1. Analyze what they are motivated by and for.
2. Write specifically what you need them to do, whether it's a project or a different way of working.
3. Craft the language you will use to motivate them.
4. Record yourself delivering the message.

Your tone needs to match your message. If team members are ethos-driven, add weight to the language by expressing a serious, almost earnest tone about who wants them to do the project or why this project is so important. If emotions move them, get excited or use an urgent tone, and they will jump. Logically motivated teammates need calm, balanced delivery of the reasons behind the work. Whatever pulls them, your tone can push them toward the work you need them to want to produce.

THE TEST

Are they meeting your deadlines? If you set your expectations and the time frame in which you need the work completed, deadlines are the ultimate metric for motivation. If your teammates are motivated, they will always meet your deadlines. They will either finish early or complete the project beyond expectations. Employees who are treading water or demotivated ask for extensions, present incomplete work, or miss deadlines completely.

Deadlines also measure whether a motivated employee has too much to do. If you know you've spoken to the person's motivation, if you've given a clear priority list of expectations and deadlines and they are still struggling, a narrower focus or partners may be needed. People who want to lead but are struggling with deadlines can signal a functional problem with workload or even weakness in the organization's overall strategy. Motivated leaders who can't succeed may be playing a game they can't win.

CHAPTER 4

FRAME

Framing is intentionally choosing words to set your listener's expectations. Leaders and managers too often say things that send the wrong message and unintentionally bring up topics that distract their teams. Organizations send out global communications that disengage their people. In this chapter, you'll learn how to choose the right language and to emphasize the parts of a message that you want your listeners to focus on.

How to Grab Your Listeners' Attention: Doug Ludwig

Every day Doug Ludwig goes to work, someone could die. As a lead guide for Adventures on the Gorge in West Virginia, he is responsible for as many as eight rafts a day as they navigate the second-oldest river in the world. He could be leading a group of kids, executives doing team building, or bikers on a bachelor party. Clients come from everywhere, and many of them have never rafted before. If they don't understand and remember Doug's instructions, the roaring water and rocks will flip the boat. Their lives will be at risk. His challenge is the same as that of any great leader: getting people to understand and remember what he says.

Everyone who goes on one of Doug's trips is as safe as you can be while doing an adventure sport because Doug frames like a master communicator. When you meet him, if he notices that you're nervous, he says, "You're in Doug's world, and this is my rodeo. Get ready to enjoy the ride." His words evoke exhilaration and risk, but then he makes the challenge approachable because he says you're in "Doug's world." Instead of his listeners fearing what's ahead, he commands their attention and sets the frame that he is in charge and confident.

He intentionally chooses words to frame his messages about safety and fun: "I start by putting people above myself. I look at what you need. I take a different approach with a football team, a group of business professionals, or a church group. But my safety speech stays the same because the more you can explain to people, the more comfortable they are." Doug gives a prepared presentation to each group, but he adjusts his language to frame the message in the way his listeners need if they are to focus. This is vital for anyone in a business environment. Do you adapt your frames to the real needs of the people in front of you?

"It's hard because people don't want to listen. They are on vacation," says Doug. "They've paid a lot of money for this trip and they want to relax. That's why I want to capture them, so that they know what's going on out here." It's no different when your people have too much to do in the office. You have to capture their attention by choosing words and phrases that remove the chaos.

After "Good morning, welcome to Class Six," he starts with the "brain bucket." He doesn't call it a helmet. "If you see your raft guide put on his brain bucket, that's a pretty good indication that you should be wearing yours, too." Of course, frames don't have to be humorous. That's Doug's style. But great frames immediately drive a memorable message into your head. You don't think going on the trip that you want to wear a helmet. You want to be free on open water. But of course rafters want to protect their brains. Who wouldn't want to be like the river guides who safely navigate raging water? Doug's frames change people's minds almost effortlessly.

His frames help rafters to stay loose. As he introduces the raft guides, he says, "These are the top of the top raft guides in the world, and this is Jimmy. Jimmy will be our bus driver. He's our third best bus driver. We have three. Jimmy used to be a raft guide, but we caught him drinking a case of beer before the trip, so now he's our bus driver." If the guides can joke about themselves, they must be the best. Again, this reinforces his listeners' confidence, helping them to continue feeling safe and to focus on Doug's message.

QUICK TEST

Did you intentionally prepare what you wanted to say before your last difficult conversation or meeting?

One of Doug's favorite frames is "participation": "The paddle is a 'participation stick.' When I'm talking about falling out of the boat, I tell people to 'participate in your rescue.' This is a participation sport, and I prepare people for how we are going to talk to them. I say, 'Your raft guides are not barking out thoughts; they are barking out commands. In the middle of a class five rapid, these are the best of the best. If you stop paddling, at that point we are not interested in your feelings. If you need a friend, get a dog.'" It's the fifth-biggest river in the world, and Doug makes sure that everyone is clear about the plan to stay in the boat.

"When we finish with safety, I let you know that you have the option to ride back on the bus, but that 'my speech was to prepare you, not to scare you.' I say that twice. I finish with three tips to keep you in the raft. 'First, brace your feet in good, but don't bend your bones. They break. Second, stick your paddle in the water when we say paddle. Reach out and meet your destiny and have control over your future. The whole idea is that we take the raft down the river, not the river taking us down. And the third tip is: you sit on a couch, you sit on a bus, you sit on a La-Z-Boy. You ride a horse, you ride a bike, and you ride the raft. You stroke, you ride. You stroke, you ride."

The best frames make your point clearly by removing language that distracts from your message. In his final instructions, Doug gives rafters one last frame so that they'll know what do on the water: "The past is history, the future is a mystery. That is why we call it the present because that's what it is, a gift. When the river is mellow, be mellow.

When it's intense, you need to be intense. It will let you know what you need to do."

Everything Doug says is an intentional metaphor that takes the fear out of the danger and emphasizes the safety and the fun. He looks at his audience and adapts to its needs. He makes sure that the words he uses convey the most important information like calling a paddle a "participation stick" and instructions like "You stroke, you ride" so that they know how to paddle. A client told him recently, "I'm not even sure how you do what you do, but you're really good at what you do." Doug is an example to every leader in any organization about the power of intentionally framing communication.

The Fourth Technique: Frame

The best frames work because they keep your listeners focused on the conversation you want to have right now or prepare them for the conversations you are going to have. The secret is to know what language will convey the message you intend so that your meaning is obvious and unforgettable.

> Frame = *understand your listeners' attitudes* + *intentional word choice* = your listeners focused on your message

If you are a leader or a manager, you have to deeply appreciate the power of your words. Every syllable that comes out of your mouth will be noticed and scrutinized. Your people will either act or fail to produce based on the language you choose.

Every word has a meaning, evokes images and ideas, and reminds people of their past experiences and values. People have attitudes about language, and they react when certain words are used. Think of the words, terms, or phrases used in your organization that evoke positive or negative impressions. Where are the places where language is being forced into your culture and is demotivating your team? The wrong word can send someone a message that you never intended, cause a meeting to go way off track, or stall an entire operation. If you choose the right language, you focus people's attention and empower them to engage in whatever is most important right now.

The Recipe

The fourth technique is for every leader to:

1. Identify the point.
2. Think about issues, ideas, or language that will distract the listener.
3. Choose vocabulary and imagery that will focus conversations and thinking.
4. Prepare the frames ahead of time.

The Method

You can't frame a conversation effectively unless you know what you're talking about. This sounds too obvious, but how many times have you walked into meetings unprepared or watched others fumble for the right words? Being prepared, however, doesn't mean that you have to have all the answers. Rather, it means that you've thought about your listeners' reactions to your words.

Framing starts with what you want to say. The language you choose depends entirely on whom you're speaking to and the relationship you're trying to build. Your frame may differ when you're speaking to someone above you or someone who works for you. It may depend on where your listener is from and his education, profession, industry, and lifestyle. Imagine beginning a meeting by describing a situation as a disaster. If one of your listeners has a spouse with cancer, he will immediately think that you don't know what disaster means. If you said, "serious situation," you would be more likely to keep his attention.

The key is preparation. Even spending a few minutes writing the frame for a conversation or the beginning of a meeting on a napkin at lunch can help you grab your listeners' attention. Why? Your listeners will hear your clarity. They will focus because your words evoke thinking. When you're framing globally—like for your team or your entire company's vision, strategy, or messaging—you should test your frames ahead of time with colleagues or with a trusted advisor. This allows you to make sure that the language sends the meaning you intend. Ask people for their best frame for an issue. You don't have to create all the right words. You only have to discover the words that will engage and motivate.

How to Frame a One-on-One Conversation

You are the director of marketing, and you want to change approach. Your boss values trade shows and conferences, even as the world changes. You know that over the few days or week of an event, you can reach only a fraction of the attendees. You want to bring a digital transformation to your business, but here's the twist. It's not in the budget.

Unfortunately, your boss is old school and wants to market the same way *he* always has: print, a static website, and if he's really feeling adventurous, email blasts. You need a strategy for helping him see that a webinar or social campaign will improve the department's results. You want him to see the potential in the change and present your ideas to the C-suite. If you say "webinar" or "social" up front, he will be defensive. It's crazy, but just one word too soon in the conversation can distract. He doesn't understand your idea's value yet.

His initial response to your request is always going to be no if you say, "I need more budget for a webinar." "More budget" is a dangerous frame because it implies cost, risk, and possible loss. Distracting with that detail before he understands the potential gain blurs the dialogue you need to create. The first frame comes in the form of a question: "Is there an interest in increasing the number of high-quality leads?" It seems too obvious, but frames have to pull the memory files that matter to the listener. Your goal is to start the conversation with what the listener cares about.

If you then say, "What if we found a way to turn the 500 leads from a trade show into 5,000 and increase the percentage of high-quality leads from 50 to 80?" You still haven't said "webinar." He will want to know how, so you keep narrowing the frame. You still don't say "webinar," but you include it. Next you say, "I have been exploring options—email blasts, contests, webinars. Email is cheap, but our success has varied recently. Contests are not expensive, and people like them. However, we've gotten feedback that people might not stay for the demo. People who register for the webinar get the demo, and we already know that they are high quality because they took the time to fill out the form. They tell us if we can send them emails in the future or not."

As you narrow down the frame connecting your idea to the one thing he wanted to talk about—leads—you have helped to reshape his perception of the word *webinar*. Now the same word means more leads. Before, it was just a new technology. Now you can talk about how to present it to the executives as a way to improve results.

In this example, our hero had an agenda. Sometimes you're framing a brainstorming session or a conversation about strategy in general rather than a specific solution. The same technique applies. You have to start with a large frame to invite the listener into the conversation, and the frame has to be an image that captures the audience's mind. Use a word that is big enough and excites. Then talk about what you want to do that will create that value. Starting wide creates room for people to engage the conversation from their perspective, which also sparks their interest and participation.

The Wrong Word Ends a Meeting

Say the wrong word, and your people's thoughts catapult into the land of worry. They will not hear anything you say because they are still stuck on the image that just erupted in their minds. For instance, if you say "layoffs," everyone in the room gets nervous. It is not dishonest to choose language that will focus your team on the real problem.

Instead, frame the conversation with, "How will we increase revenue in order to prevent having to cut our expenses?" Keep the focus on how to bring money in even as you talk about expense cutting. If you use layoffs as a threat, do it because you've thought things through and are confident that this is the best frame for your conversation. For terms that create fear and urgency, if they aren't used in the right context, your people will leave the meeting ready to search for a new job instead of focusing on the problem.

How Will You Fire a Teammate?

Saying, "You're fired" works for celebrities on television, sort of. In an organization where you want to build trust among your team, however, what matters is how you help your poor performers move on. Your team members are watching you. They will notice how you let someone go. When an employee is not meeting expectations and is dragging down morale, if you wait too long, you hurt your team. Coldly removing someone doesn't work either, even when the person deserves it. There are environments in which a public dismissal to instill fear can work, but your organization has to be the unique environment in which this is appropriate. If you wonder whether your organization is that kind of environment, it probably isn't. When a culture is draconian, you know it, and it's that way on purpose.

Once you know the legal frames that you have to use, understand why the person is no longer right for the company. You've already heard frames like "This is no longer a good fit," and "The organization is going in another direction," and these are better than "You're fired." But the best frames are about the person's future direction and his talent. You want him to succeed, even if he's been driving you crazy and you don't really like him. You want him to be in an organization where his talents make the company better.

He might even call you and thank you for setting him free if you say:

> "I want you to find an organization where you get the appreciation you deserve."

> "You need your ability to (name his talent) to get the support we can't give you."

> "I want you to find an organization where your talent meets the organization's needs."

You're not sugarcoating the message or lying when you help someone focus on images of future success. If you haven't given him feedback about why he has been underperforming, the moment when you end his employment is too late. Taking the time to frame well and making an effort to refocus the discomfort raises your ethos during a difficult situation. It also sends the message to your team members that you take their careers seriously.

The exception is when you fire someone for illegal behavior like theft. Even in that case, the person was "dismissed" when you are talking with her peers. Again, check the legal differences, and then use the frame that will reveal to the rest of your team members that you are a leader who values them, as you are a manager who wants only teammates who perform.

Framing Change

When implementing a change management effort, maximize motivation because people will struggle with the new situation. Some people in your organization won't like what's happening, even if it's positive. Change causes stress. When people are stressed, they may not see the good in the new world if it feels too big. Your communication has to focus their thoughts about the new reality. For instance, you can't simply send an email saying that you're going to merge sales and marketing starting next month. It's not enough. You have to frame the change in a way that will keep people motivated. You have to add additional information, but as you do it, you have to reach out to the different ways people need information.

The change has to be imminent if a change effort is to be successful. You have to add something like, "The Board pushed us to lower our expenses. As an alternative to layoffs, by consolidating sales and marketing, we will minimize cost and improve collaboration." If your response is, "Of course you'd say something like that"—brilliant, but do you know what not to say?

You could have said many things that not only won't work but also will create new problems.

1. "We're merging sales and marketing next month."
2. "The Board told us to merge sales and marketing, and it will happen next month."
3. "The Board is not happy with our performance as a company and has instructed us to find ways to cut our costs. Therefore, we're going to merge sales and marketing."

These are all negative. They are not going to motivate. For a change effort to be successful, your message has to come from the top. It has to be focused and energizing, not casual. It has to contain the logic that explains the change. These three motivations from the matrix push people, and change is an essential moment to apply their energy. Everyone has to adopt the frame for the change to become a natural part of your culture.

Framing Global Communication in Your Organization

You've just learned about how to frame conversations as an individual leader and manager (in Chapter 8 we'll talk in more detail about how to frame meetings). In addition to its use in your daily work with people, framing is also a challenge for global communication. Too many organizations don't do it well.

Global communications include everything from emails about what's happening in the organization, messages in marketing and sales language, and even presentations or trainings about the kind of behaviors you want out of every member of your team. Organizations drop bombs on their people without thinking about how those messages will land. Frames that some level of management wants their people to use consistently are forced on teams below, and you as the leader or manager are left to clean up the mess.

Too often framing of vision, processes, and how to work together feels disconnected from the reality of efforts on the front lines. Every one of your people comes to work with different experiences and attitudes about how he can be effective. When the framing in your organization doesn't feel authentic, your people will struggle, then disengage, and then start doing their own thing.

When you frame global communication that you want to be consistent throughout your team or your organization, even if you're managing only a few people, start by getting the people closest to you on board. Whether one-on-one or with a group off-site, whether you create the frames together or use your team to test and refine the language, invite a conversation about the language. You are not selling; you are crafting sticky memory files that matter.

You can't dictate the adoption of language: that's propaganda. To get buy-in, you need to find the two most important people on your team: the influencer and the critic. You know the person whom other people listen to, and you know the person who will be judgmental of everything. You need their buy-in—because they either helped choose, helped test, or simply approved the language as your trusted advisors. When they care, others will too.

Sometimes you can create global communications as a team and with large parts of your organization. Other times a small group has to do the framing. Either way, the value of global framing is the same as that of having any conversation where you want people to focus. Know your point, remove the language that distracts, and intentionally choose words and images that emphasize the ideas that you want understood or considered.

How to Reframe Your Company: Scott McCallum

The Aidmatrix Foundation is one of the most powerful sources of generosity in the world. Every year, it works with more than 50,000 organizations—governments, corporations, and humanitarian agencies—to deliver billions of dollars in relief aid that affects the lives of tens of millions of people. It's been able to have dumbfounding impact, and part of the reason is how it frames what it does.

Scott McCallum, former governor of Wisconsin, became CEO and president in 2005 and served for nine years. At the time that he joined, the organization had a perception problem. McCallum recalled:

The most difficult issue is *technology* itself. Even the word *technology* tends to be cold. It's not a feeling word. So the problem we had was taking the word *technology* and the purpose of the organization and making it matter to people.

The first week, I tried to change some of the marketing. I asked questions to people who had never been asked. I got everyone together. I had a homework assignment for everyone. "You get a one-line statement on public radio. Describe what we do." Everyone had to do it, including the tech people, who had never been asked before. They came up with tremendous ideas.

The second exercise I did was to ask, "You've worked here a few years, and your mother asks you what you do. What do you tell your mother Aidmatrix does?" They learned very quickly that we needed to change from a technology culture to a team culture. This is our mission. We are helping people.

With additional help from an outside firm, Aidmatrix changed from talking about technology to declaring itself a "team of passionate people . . . dedicated to creating and delivering tools and processes that bring people together to help others." While what it technically does is use supply chain management and Internet technology to get food, medical supplies, and money to people in need, the message is warmer when it's framed as "Aidmatrix links aid with need worldwide."

Instead of talking about computer systems, teammates talk about their work in terms of partnerships with the people who get help and the people helping disaster victims, the hungry, and the sick. "We didn't talk about what *we* can do. Our objective was to magnify their mission, to improve the good works they do. The work we did was as a partner. . . . We wanted to help the people be better at what *they* do."

The results of paying attention to how to frame the message were staggering. McCallum said that after reframing Aidmatrix "had 400 percent growth in four years in terms of the amount of aid we moved through the system and the number of people we've helped. This was built with no one in sales, and we had one person marketing eight hours a week. Aidmatrix have shareholders needing a profit. The shareholders are people who don't have a lot of resources. The message is so important because anybody who uses the product is the sales force. People who work with the company are so committed to what it does and find it works so well that they become its best salespeople."

Aidmatrix continued to find the right language for what it did because its people spent time with their partners. "Part of our annual meeting was that we went on-site with one of the organizations we worked with," noted McCallum. "For example, we visited one of our food bank partners to see the good things it was doing. That brings home what we do."

And what Aidmatrix does is not always easy. The areas where its "mankind information systems" can help include disaster relief, hunger, free medical clinics, and virtual aid drives to raise money. The funds and products—like getting food, water, and diapers into a disaster area—come from three different constituencies: nonprofits like churches and the Red Cross, for-profit corporations, and governments. Each organization had had its own system for helping people, and they had never been integrated before. McCallum said that "this is a tough business because we are change agents. Any time there is change, you are pushing people into a discomfort zone."

So Aidmatrix worked just as hard on the framing internally. "We broke down the culture and shared information," said McCallum. "I talked with people informally whenever I could, and as you grow as an organization, you have to work harder and harder at it. When we were small enough, we could have a weekly meeting that included everybody, but it became just the executive team. Even that happened only once a month because of travel." The frames have to be consistent so that they reach people across the globe.

Teammates used every means of communication to keep the culture open and information clear and memorable. McCallum observed, "People could send emails to all employees. I would come in very early on Thursdays to call the global directors around the world. They got a chance to talk directly with me. It's important to have that communication time. I shared the stories of how it was going in D.C. or of my meeting with the World Bank. I have a rule that you never get in trouble for telling me something, no matter how small it may be. You never get in trouble for giving me too much information. We kept track of it all on Google Groups and salesforce.com. If the CEO's plane goes down, the organization shouldn't."

How to Build Relationships for Crisis: Tom Endersbe

Ameriprise Financial has 10,000 advisors, and the frames that advisors use to build long-term relationships are critical. Economic turbulence in the global economy is normal. In the fall of 2008, five of the ten biggest single-day declines in the history of the Dow Jones Industrial Average happened in a period from September 29 to October 22. These enormous losses happened just as the first in the baby boom generation, the 450 million citizens worldwide born between 1943 and the mid-1960s, prepared to retire. What can an advisor say to a client to maintain the relationship in the face of huge losses in the client's portfolio?

As vice president of marketing sales strategies, field communications, and training for Ameriprise Financial at the time, Tom Endersbe and his team were responsible for collecting and creating the frames that advisors across America used to connect with their 2.8 million clients. It is Endersbe's genuine interest in what people need that prepared him for this challenge.

His experience in framing messages that build relationships began in his youth when he sold seeds door-to-door to buy a pup tent. Notice his framing when people opened the door: "Hi, my name is Tom, and I live down the street. I've always noticed you working in your yard, and I'm here to sell seeds. But first I'd love to have you tell me about your garden." Because they told him about their horticultural secrets, after they took him to show off their favorite vegetables, he could say, "I have some really great seeds from a great company. I'd love to show you and see if there is anything in your garden that you don't have today." This may feel too simple as language, but wait for the punchline. Reflecting back,

Tom said, "People would tell me what they wanted from me, and I'd simply give it to them." Tom was seven. Imagine if every teammate in your organization had authentic language to explore customers' needs.

In Ameriprise's work, financial meltdowns make the work of financial advisors feel impossible. There are right words in almost every situation. For advisors to be effective, they have to know the frames to begin conversations, the best ways to describe the available strategies, and the language that supports an ongoing relationship, especially as clients struggle. In crisis and ordinary time, Endersbe said, "The challenge was in enrolling our distributors, advisors, and corporate employees in changing to learn these patterns of effective communication."

Endersbe learned the reason that framing is so important as a salesman for Maytag. The new hires went through a boot camp three-month training. For two months, they gave presentations and sales meetings and sold everything but washing machines. In their final exercise, they were given a Kenmore and a Maytag in separate rooms. All their pieces were lying on the floor, and the trainees had to put them together. They were both white boxes. The goal was to teach every salesperson what it was on the inside that made Maytag extraordinary. Tom became the number one salesperson in two regions.

Feeling that there was more to life than washing machines, Endersbe went to work for IDS, the company purchased by American Express in 1984 that became Ameriprise Financial Services in 2005. He built the top district in the nation, and went on to help every advisor connect with their clients more consistently:

> I told my story to advisors when I wanted them to understand that when you're an advocate for the person you're seeking to understand, there are no limits. It is always about the other person. Every piece of material should be in the spirit of this kind of interaction. So many times we send or provide information that isn't around a common process, and so the noise is so loud that in the confusion of the format, people can't hear what's in there.

Ameriprise has always been successful, but its advisors had not used the same language to build relationships with clients. Endersbe mentioned that "in the past, Ameriprise had 20 sales models. Before we rebuilt the common language, there were nine in use. All of them were great, but they were inconsistent. The inconsistency affected execution. No one was delivering consistent messages."

Endersbe listened to the needs of advisors all over the country, and, using his experience running the most successful office, he gave frames to connect with clients, particularly in times when they are suffering. He said that "when advisors followed our Dream>Plan>Track> process, they could help shape a view of money for a lifetime. Not only does every advisor have a disciplined process of financial planning, but they all serve clients through intentional regular, frequent interaction. They start with dreams and move to creating and defining a plan that builds and tracks a person's dream."

The frame, "disciplined process of financial planning," is only five words, but it takes into account the uncertainty of investing and creates comfort about the security of an Ameriprise professional. The Dream>Plan>Track> model spoke not only to emotional hopes, but also to a sturdy, logical approach that will weather any market storms. Every financial advisor used this language. Responding to the crisis, for example, advisors started by listening to their clients, and then saying, "Ameriprise was built for times like these. So was your plan. Now, more than ever, you need a plan." The language is direct, focused on the client's anxiety and what the advisor can do because of his talent and the strong organization behind him.

Ameriprise offers its advisors weekly training and has e-learning available 24/7, offering the frames that help advisors feel confident when building trusting relationships with clients. Endersbe noted that "we had a distribution process for methods—written materials, podcasts, and live broadcasts—where our advisors trained on the core concepts and communication methodologies, from the basics of communication up to the tax law of the strategic solution. We targeted the sophistication of the top 20 percent with our new language. We took complex ideas and made it so that every advisor could learn them at any level. We brought our advisors to another level of consciousness about their relationships with clients."

How to Frame Consistent Communication with Clients: Wendy Miller

As chief marketing officer at Bain & Company, a global management consulting firm, Wendy Miller oversaw framing how consultants engage clients until 2018. Every one of the firm's more than 10,000 employees that generate billions in yearly income approaches clients the same way. As the head of diamond giant De Beers told the *Financial Times*, he had to hire Bain rather than the other top consulting firms because it would give "the most uncomfortable ride." Bain's reputation for direct, result-focused engagements differentiates it. What's remarkable is how clearly Bain reinforces this culture with new employees in extensive orientation programs, which include specific material about the Bain Voice and how to "Communicate for Results."

Miller related how her personal history with Bain led her to help create the communication methodology: "I joined Bain in 1984 out of college. It was such a unique place, focused on results, not just analysis. This seemed not only much more rewarding, but also more fun. After business school, I came back to Bain and worked part-time for a while to focus on my young family. While I never thought I'd stay as long as I did, I came for the people, and I stayed for the people. Bain's people are what make it such a special culture."

Consistently voted best consultancy to work for, Bain uses frames to help consultants communicate consistently with clients, which emerged from its original culture. As Miller observed: "We were founded in 1973, and in 1998 we realized that we needed to reflect our brand more systematically in our communication style. As a firm, we were distinct in our culture and with our people, but to the rest of the world, we hid our personality because we were afraid of looking too different."

In 2000, the firm created the Bain Voice. The Bain Voice is not a language. It frames the direct, jargon-free style that consultants use in every conversation, email, or publication. It originally started with the editorial team. Miller guided its extension throughout the company because Bain's brand is conveyed in each interaction with everyone, from recruits to clients. "Bain doesn't advertise, so their reputation is about their people and making sure that they communicate in a way that reflects who they are," Miller said. "The editorial team developed it, trying to create a unique style of writing that reflected Bain's brand. We soon realized that this should apply to all interactions and touch points, not just articles."

Bain has 58 offices in 37 countries. With this global reach, a client hiring a team in London could also be working with Bain teams in New York and Beijing. To achieve consistency, as part of their training, consultants joining the company receive two slides. The first frames the content, structure, and style of every communication—ideas like "outlines with no more than four points," "answer first format," and "cut out jargon." The second is a 105-word description of what it is like when you meet the Bain Voice. One line is the most memorable: "If you met the Bain Voice at a cocktail party, you'd be happy to talk with him." This method of teaching the Bain Voice works because it is as direct and clear as the firm's engagements with clients.

New employees are introduced to the Bain Voice in an hour-long presentation, and it is reinforced because it is the behavior of every employee. It also becomes an integral expectation in their performance. Miller noted:

We had operating principles that we measured people on. We had twice a year performance reviews, and we wanted to know if our people are living our operating principles. Bain has its own internal language, but it isn't used with clients. It does not help to spew academic, jargon-ridden advice. Bain hires down-to-earth, pragmatic people who want to roll up their sleeves and have fun along the way. That's an important way the firm makes a difference with clients.

It was essential that all of us spoke in language that was not intimidating, but that was inclusive and action-oriented. If communication isn't clear, it risks clients not understanding and acting upon advice. The Bain Voice is answer first, and backs up the messages with data. That makes it harder for clients to miss hearing the tough messages.

PRACTICE THE TECHNIQUE

Drill: Writing It Out

You have to deliver a difficult message, set clear expectations, or shape the focus of a group. Don't think that because you understand the issues, you are ready. That's just the first step. What frames will convey the message you intend and focus your listeners on the meaning you want them to remember?

1. Write down the point.
2. List the negative words and phrases that will distract your listener.
3. List memorable images, the words and phrases that emphasize your point.
4. Write your message, inductively or deductively to match your listener's tendency, avoiding the distraction words and phrases and using your most memorable images.
5. Test the frames with a trusted advisor.

Whether framing a one-on-one conversation, a meeting, or a global message to your company or the world, the process is the same. The question is: Who helps ensure that your perceptions are accurate? Coaching one person's performance improvement or a small team's understanding of a new challenge, you probably only need to test your frames with one trusted advisor. When the number of people impacted by your framing increases, create a focus group that knows the environment and can contribute to the process of choosing the right words.

THE TEST

Do they use your language? In a well-framed conversation, whether one-on-one or in a large presentation, your listeners can tell you what they heard. If your frame is effective, they will use the same words you do when they are talking to you after the conversation. If you want to influence people above and below you, you have to be consistent and intentional with the words you use to describe your core process and product as well as the way you want people to work together. When people start using your frames, you have focused their attention. They know what you need them to do, and they know the reasons why.

CHAPTER 5

VALIDATE

Validation is acknowledging that you have heard and appreciated another person's participation. If you're leading or managing and you don't validate, your teammates will disengage because they don't feel that their contributions matter. Validation is rarely as simple as saying, "Good job." In this chapter, you will learn why validating is important in every arena and how to validate without sounding inauthentic.

The Fifth Technique: Validate

Validation is much more than a pat on the back. Whether you are talking with executives or with the people who work with you, they need to know that what they do matters. People who work for you definitely need to know you value what they do. Even people who are not formally seeking validation need to know that their efforts are recognized. With customers, this may mean being heard. With colleagues, it may mean being accepted. With people who report to you, it may mean knowing that they are on the right track.

Validation = affirming the other person's value

Validation is not babying, pandering, or sucking up. It doesn't mean agreeing with the other person. Validation is helping the other person understand why he matters so he can focus on being successful.

Validation is the technique that develops relationships. With the right validation, you will be able to withstand conflict, provide feedback, and foster a productive and creative environment. Whether your organization is large or small, how do your people know that they are doing the right work? They need to know that they are going in the direction that you believe will lead to success. Validation allows people to understand their role and feel committed to their projects.

The Recipe

Validation can be as simple as a head nod or saying, "That's a good question" in a meeting. When you validate, either one-on-one or in a group session, people engage. If you're in a meeting, they'll participate. Internals who think before they talk will come by after the meeting and start sharing their ideas. In a big group, the room will buzz. The fifth technique for every leader is to:

1. Listen to the message and meaning of what the person is saying.
2. Analyze what the other person sees as effective validation.
3. Formulate a response that acknowledges the person's contributions without judgment.

The Method

Are you good at listening? Listening is not agreeing; it is taking in someone's words, both the logical meaning and the emotion behind the communication, and appreciating the message. It is paying attention to the person and processing what he says. If he thinks you're not listening, he will either ignore you, get angry, or keep repeating himself.

Over time, you will learn how each of the members of your team needs validation. You can't validate effectively unless you understand where someone is coming from. Building that strong relationship begins by figuring out what each person needs. Some people need you to just listen, others need to brainstorm. As ironic as it may sound, the best way to validate some members of your team is to leave them alone.

QUICK TEST

Do your people think you are a good listener?

How They Want to Feel Heard

One-on-One

You were an emergency room doctor. You ran the fast-paced, direct, immediate response in the ER. Now you've been promoted into management, and you're not in the middle of the fire. You oversee 150 professionals in different areas. You've been with the organization for 15 years, and one of your favorite colleagues has been there for 25. Now he reports to you.

He's in charge of one of the weekly reports that helps your staff members schedule their teams for the next week. He's supposed to complete the work on Wednesday so that changes can be made before the weekend. Not only is he not including you in the process, but he's not following the required protocols. When you approach him, he says, "The report's useless. It's not like anyone reads it. People do what they want."

In this case, the behavior needs to change. Most of us struggle to make adjustments if we don't feel valued first. A normal and natural reaction when you first get the leadership role is to threaten him with consequences if he doesn't start preparing the report right. Instead, you take a validating approach. As you sit down with him at your next update, you begin by saying, "Tell me the history of how you came to do these reports this way." When you listen, you will hear the real reasons because there is no threat to your colleague.

By validating with asking and listening, even though you're frustrated, he will see in your demeanor that you want to make the situation better. If you finish the validation by paraphrasing what he just said, he can confirm you are on the same page. Once you've clarified that you hear his approach, you can talk to him about what needs to be different and he can hear why.

In a Meeting

You're in a departmentwide meeting, and you've just finished a presentation on a new policy concerning health insurance offerings. You're the department head, and one of your employees asks you about a better healthcare plan for families. You already know that there isn't money in the budget to invest in the plan your teammate is requesting. How do you say no so that he doesn't disengage?

You might say, "Colby, give me an example of what you'd like to see different." Right there, the fact that you've expressed an interest in his question has validated his need.

Colby replies, "Our family just had a new baby, and I'm wondering if we can increase the benefits for pediatric care."

Pause to make sure Colby is done, then respond to him and the entire room by saying, "What Colby just said is very important and affects a number of us. I am glad this was brought up so that we can talk about it." Now you've validated Colby, and you can answer the question. "We're not going to change it this quarter, but I'll bring your feedback to the executives as we talk about the rest of the year." If you suspect anyone needs further validation, invite people to speak to you later.

An Angry Listener in Front of a Group

A heckler, an angry colleague, or someone who is just having a really bad day is trying to get your attention. You want to ignore him, but you can't. At a certain point he has the attention of the people in the room, and you have to decide how to defuse it. Validation is still the answer.

On the very last day of Ronald Reagan's 1980 campaign for the presidency, in his very final event, the lights were not working. It was late. He was exhausted. In a frustrated, but not angry tone, he told the heckler, "Ah, shut up." The moment he said the words, he smiled. The crowd went crazy. Reagan was known as the great communicator because he could get away with that kind of retort. This worked for Reagan because he had the ethos as a presidential candidate and an emotionally charged crowd that loved him. Most of us have to spend a bit more time and use a few more words to quell this type of situation.

Barack Obama used multiple approaches at a speech in Chicago, and you can apply all of them. The protest was a coordinated attack by at least three angry individuals in the audience. One of them started screaming. Then the others started chanting too. For a public speaker, distraction is hard enough. Anger stops most of us from thinking clearly. Obama looked at the loudest protester and listened. He just listened.

Then, after the person paused to take a breath, he said, "Okay, I've heard you." They didn't stop. Another protester started talking. Obama listened again. Then he said, "Hold on. Don't just start yelling." When the third protester began again, he smiled and raised his hand. In a calm voice, using the microphone, he said, "I've listened to you." He didn't stop there. He looked and gestured at each of the three people, saying, "I heard you, I heard you, and I heard you."

And they kept screaming. He said, "No one is removing you. I've heard you, but you have to listen to me, too. I understand that you may disagree, but we have to be able to talk honestly about these issues." When they kept going, he finally shut them down when he said, "It's good to be back in Chicago." The crowd laughed. He finished, "Because everyone has something to say."

The validation happened consistently in multiple places. First, he stopped talking when the screaming began and listened. Second, he made eye contact with the protesters. He validated their voice without giving them control. Third, he acknowledged that he heard them. Fourth, he indicated that he was willing to have dialogue. That brief dialogue truly validated them, and while the protesters might not have been satisfied, the rest of the crowd saw his self-control and caring for every voice.

If you face someone who is angry, address the person. Listen as he makes his point. Interject if he starts to be redundant or too ridiculous, and then respond. As you listen, look at or walk toward the person. Don't violate his personal space. Instead, show that you are not afraid. Asking him to continue does not mean that you agree with him. It gives you the chance to address him directly and shows that you are a confident, unflappable leader. When he is done or has gone on long enough, walk away and redirect the conversation. In most cases, you just took the room back by validating.

How You Get Good at Listening

While we know listening is essential, do you know how to do it? Could you teach others? Listening may be all the validation a teammate needs. These guidelines are the best practice for being an effective listener.

1. *Get ready like an athlete.* Mentally and physically, you have to choose to be in the moment and engage. If email distracts you, turn off the computer. If you're worrying about other issues, write them down so you can tackle them later.
2. *Control bias.* You have filters and judgments based on people's ethos. These get in the way. If you know that you don't like someone or don't trust him, admit this ahead of time so you don't shut down during the conversation. Shutting down translates into not caring, and not caring makes it impossible to accurately understand what the other person is saying.
3. *Separate fact and feeling.* "Last quarter we had to lay off 400 people from the company" is a technical comment, whereas "Man, we had to lay off 400" is an emotional response. Determining whether someone is speaking about facts or about feelings is a listening skill. What you say next is very different in the two cases. You can talk about facts with interest and curiosity. But if someone is expressing emotion, the only validation that matters at first is something like, "That's tough," with a compassionate tone.
4. *Pick up cue words.* A cue word indicates which way the conversation is going. If you're a daydreamer, you listen for when someone says, "The bottom line here is." That's a cue that he's about to give the core of his message. Other examples like "What we need to do here" or "What I'm trying to say is" also indicate that the person is about to deliver the punch line.

"In conclusion" or "To sum it all up" means that the person is going to deliver the message you need to remember.

Different Kinds of Validation

The best validation is simple, but creative. For instance, if you're an executive, the very act of popping by the office or sitting down in the cube of someone who has a more junior title validates his membership on the team. You don't have to say, "I'm proud of you," or "You're doing great work." Just the fact that you, the leader, are sitting down with him tells him that he is important.

Sometimes to validate, you may need to have an entire conversation where you listen to someone vent and don't even bring up the issues you really want to talk about. This gesture is powerful and demonstrates that you value this person beyond just his technical skills. With the trust you've built, the next time you need to meet with him to discuss your points, usually he will have an easier time listening and understanding, no matter what the topic.

Validating effectively is about noticing a person's contribution to a conversation, a meeting, or a team. If you do this enough at the beginning of a relationship, later you may not have to validate at the beginning of the conversation. But if someone doesn't feel validated, you don't have trust. Some common validators are:

1. *Offering stock phrases.* When you say something like "Good job" or "Great question," if your tone says the same thing, it can be enough to value someone's work. If the stock phrase feels too short, add "because" and offer the reason the person is successful.
2. *Paraphrasing the message.* Paraphrasing is evidence that you heard the person's words. Paraphrase not only the words but also the tone.
3. *Asking a meaningful question.* Your interest in digging deeper demonstrates that the person said something that has enough merit that you want to know more.

4. **Telling a story about the person's success.** Check motivation. You may not want to tell the story in public, but even in a one-on-one meeting, mentioning a person's past achievement affirms his work and clarifies what you want him to do again and again.

5. **Using body language.** A head nod, a smile, or a wink can be dangerous if it's misinterpreted, but an appropriate nod or thumbs-up can be all the other person needs in a meeting to let him know that he is doing the right things.

6. **Employing your physical presence.** If you are the leader and you show up at someone's presentation, it shows that what that person is doing is important.

7. **Listening.** We really mean it. If you can't, won't, or don't listen, the other kinds of validation don't matter, and you should perhaps begin exploring jobs where you're not working with people.

The Word *But*

Abigail walks into her office in the morning and says to her colleague, "Paula, I really like that new hairstyle, but . . ." What's coming? It won't be good, and Abigail won't remember the compliment. You may have spent five minutes telling a teammate how much you value her role in the company and that you believe she has a bright future—then you said, "but." Everything you just said is deleted. *But* is an erasure word. It erases what you said before, and it makes your listener wonder whether you really mean what you're saying. How can someone trust you if your validation comes with conditions?

Starting with validation builds trust, and when you use connective language like *and* or *so* instead of *but*, it allows you to deliver negative feedback, the next challenge for the person to take on, or a different direction that you want her to pursue. The person hears you because you valued her first. That doesn't mean that you need to get rid of the word *but*. It means that when you're giving negative feedback or in emotionally charged situations, don't use the word.

Every Conversation, Every Meeting, Every Day

Their Idea Doesn't Get Picked

You have a brilliant brainstorming session about a new solution for dealing with a bug in your new software. You have 10 people from three departments. At the end you have an answer. But it's not everyone's answer. Now what?

If you say, "Great job, team," it could be enough. The people will value the fact that you called them a team, and they will feel good about what got done—unless they don't.

What about the person who provided his best ideas, but they weren't the ideas that you or the group chose? You can still validate him, too. Say, "What I love most about this group is that you're fearless. You're putting great ideas on the table that inspired a great solution. Thank you, everyone, for contributing." In group settings, you can't validate just the people whose ideas get picked. Valuing everyone and their part of the process creates a culture where effort matters as much as winning. Validating the process continues the momentum and energy for next time.

A Different Culture

If you do something to offend your listener, apologize. The most important thing is intention. In Japan, you may offend if you sit down in the wrong place. In China, you may offend if you fail to bow deeply enough to a CEO. In Texas, you may offend if your handshake is weak. If you are an American man dealing with a businesswoman in a Muslim country, she may not shake your hand. She doesn't want to offend you, but she doesn't know what to do because she does not physically interact with men in public. In an international environment, the best validation is to express your interest and intention to be respectful of the customs and norms of that culture.

The Difference Between Validating and Agreeing

Many managers don't validate because they fear that their validation indicates their agreement with a poor decision or point. It's not the same. There is a big difference between saying, "That's a good idea" and, "I'm glad you're bringing that idea into the discussion." The first example emphasizes the quality of the idea, good or bad. The second emphasizes the fact that the person contributed and promotes the behavior. The simple validation encourages further participation both from that person and from others.

Great leaders take risks. The people around you who want to lead will make mistakes as their leadership and management matures. You don't have to agree with them. Agreeing means that you think they have the right idea. Validating is showing respect for someone's having an idea and spending time thinking about it.

How to Show People How Good They Are: Mike Phalen

When Mike Phalen served as president of Boston Scientific's endoscopy business, he constantly managed conflicting interests and demands. A leading global provider of flexible devices to help physicians manage gastrointestinal diseases, the company's global revenue has grown to over $10 billion annually. As president, he reported to the executive team. He was responsible for his organization's products, for helping his team navigate the needs of corporate management, and for managing the resources shared among six divisions. One of his secrets: validation.

"I start out my one-on-ones by asking, 'How are you feeling?' Not 'How are you doing?'" said Phalen. "If someone needs a venting session, I want her to do it with me in a safe harbor, and because of my title, I have to let people know that it's safe to vent here." Building trust is about creating an authentic relationship at a level that works for you. People will feed off your comfort level. If you're comfortable, that validates that you are someone who is worth talking to and who really wants to know what they think.

Phalen always looks for his people's best ideas. He waits for the moment when he can show them how good they are and validate their role in the organization:

I learned an awful lot by going to the cafeteria. Sitting with a table of folks from marketing and communications, I was talking about the conference from the week before when one of the guys leaned over and said, "I got good news." That resulted in a 15-minute technical download that I would have had to go to another meeting to get.

But when we go to our project review next week, if that guy is there and he doesn't contribute, I'd put him on the spot and say, "You and I chatted last week about your perspective on this technical breakthrough. Why don't you share with the group what you told me?" This is not only to get the information shared and get it across to the group in a way that invites contribution and feedback, but also to validate that this is the guy who owns this franchise.

The best validation is deeper than saying, "Good job." It is engaging the intellectual and emotional energy of your team.

Phalen remembers people's success so that later he can build their confidence, and the fact that he remembers is powerful. For example, he recalled:

I was in Europe, and on a Sunday morning we had a global kickoff meeting. We had a young territory manager who had just taken an assignment in Spain. It was his first time at the meeting, and before I gave the keynote, the internal marketing manager recognized him. I thought, "What a great chance to connect with this guy." I changed my opening on the spot. I said, "Before I get started, I want to take a moment to formally congratulate you on your promotion and your move to Spain," then I told a story about him—this is in front of 100 people from outside the United States.

Before a national sales meeting three years earlier, we were about to play golf. He was the sales rep for this area of the country. I was ready to play golf, and he comes down the hotel stairs in a suit, and he's going to make a sales call. I leaned over and said to one of the other execs I was with, "This guy is going to go a long way." Three years later, here he is. Two nights later I had dinner with him, and he couldn't believe that I remembered him, and he was extraordinarily grateful that I'd called that out.

When you are a leader or manager with strong ethos, this kind of validation can instill confidence that lasts for that employee's career.

Phalen is just as effective with teams. "I was in our manufacturing plant, and I was addressing the senior management," he remembered. "This is a manufacturing plant in the middle of nowhere that's getting beat up by the corporate demands on a daily basis, and I wanted to tell those guys why they are important. We brought in patient success stories and talked about why the managers' leadership makes a difference."

When you show people the results of their good work, they know their value. With their trust in the work you are doing together, you can be a more aggressive leader. Because Phalen worked with the leaders on the success they had produced, he felt that "this gave me the right to ask them to do more. I always have to pace the validation, and then be able to engage that group in a way that pushes them, appreciates them, and then pushes them again."

Phalen connected people across the organization because he pays attention to what is most important in their work. "I made it a habit to validate and appreciate what each functional group brings," he says. "I have influence, but not control. The way to get influence is to validate each group's role and contribution." Phalen pointed out that, with his influence, he created an environment in which people validate each other because they speak in a way that every member of the team can understand:

I tried to understand the technical issue, and then I often defused a situation by saying, "I'm not an engineer, but I know a little bit about the process and the product. Can you break it down into layman's terminology so we can all understand?" The technical guys at BSC are extremely good at the engineering side, but that's not what's going to get the organization to accept their project. My single biggest job was to be the one who connected the dots.

PRACTICE THE TECHNIQUE

Drill 1: Using Stock Phrases

You will sound disingenuous if the phrase comes out with a tone that doesn't match what you mean. Even worse, doing so makes it sound as if you're not listening, and your ethos will drop. Here's how to practice.

1. Develop a list of stock phrases like
   "That's helpful to hear."
   "I appreciate that."
   "That's important information."
2. Practice these phrases so that you can deliver them comfortably and authentically.
3. Add the word *because* at the end of each stock phrase, and fill in the blank.

If you appreciate the reason why the stock phrase is true, your voice will reflect it (see Chapter 6 to learn more about tone). Whether the reason is emotional, logical, or reflecting back what the person has just said, he'll follow your lead when he knows that you're paying attention to his work.

Drill 2: Focusing Your Own Thoughts

It's really easy to be thinking about what you're going to say next and not really listening to what the other person is saying. To stay focused:

1. Keep an outline of your conversation or of the meeting on paper.
2. When you hear something you want to validate, circle it.
3. Start your comments with a paraphrase of that point.

People will notice your attention, and that will keep them engaged in the conversation.

THE TEST

Are they energized? If you validate effectively, people's eyes will usually light up. But remember, depending on their personality, the way they will show their excitement will vary. They may smile subtly. Or if someone is the contrarian on your team, he may simply—for the first time in weeks—not disagree. And if the person is one of the external communicators on your team, he will be excited, he will respond quickly, and his eyes will smile.

You can even deliver bad news and have it be a valuable experience. If you lead by consistently giving people a chance to feel good about what they've done, who they are, and what you believe they can do, your challenge can be their opportunity. Even if you change something—staff size, privileges, budget—if you validate people, they can recover more quickly and be ready for what's next.

CHAPTER 6

ADD COLOR

Adding color changes the sound of a word to draw attention to its meaning. Too many leaders and managers send mixed messages with the way they speak. They say something important and don't sound sincere, or they sound too excited about a topic that's not a big deal. In this chapter you will learn how to match what you say with how you say it.

How Do You Yell at a Three-Year-Old?

Your three-year-old son is chasing a ball into the street. You have to yell at him to stop. How will you say it? Try this first. In your normal conversational voice, say, "Stop."

Seriously. Unless you're in a car that someone else is driving, say it out loud. You need to feel how it sounds. Say it one more time.

Listen to your voice. Hear your natural volume and tone.

Now imagine that your child is in danger of being struck by a car if you don't get him to stop right now. Unless you are on a plane, say, "Stop!" like his life depends on it. Can you feel the difference?

What changed?

Something changed physically in how you spoke. If you can recall the difference between your natural voice and the extreme ends of your range, you can use it in other settings.

This is the technical part of how you communicate at work. Aristotle understood that no matter what you are saying, how you say it makes the difference between success and failure:

> Still, the whole business of rhetoric being concerned with appearances, we must pay attention to the subject of delivery, unworthy though it is, because we cannot do without it. The right thing in speaking really is that we should be satisfied not to annoy our hearers, without trying to delight them: we ought in fairness to fight our case with no help beyond the bare facts: nothing, therefore, should matter except the proof of those facts. Still, as has been already said, other things affect the result considerably, owing to the defects of our hearers. (*On Rhetoric*, Book III, Chapter 1, 1404a.)

Aristotle found delivery unworthy because he wanted the content to determine whether what you said won an argument. He also knew that this isn't reality.

We are easily swayed by a speaker's charisma. We are too often more impressed with the swagger of a speaker than with the substance of the message. That makes your delivery all the more important if you want to be an effective leader. The most powerful message in the world, backed up by data that proves your idea, will produce the best results. But it can still fall flat. If your delivery is poor, you will fail.

The Sixth Technique: Add Color

The science of speech communication has two physical dimensions: voice and speech. Voice is the sound that you are able to produce when air travels through your vocal cords. Speech is what you do with your voice. There is not a lot you can do to change your voice. It takes an immense amount of specific exercise, like targeting muscles at the gym. Few busy people have time to put in the work. Adding color is about controlling your speech. With the voice you have, you can have so much more impact when you intentionally craft the way you speak.

The Recipe

The final technique for mastering communication at work, the one that, like the brightest spot on a painting attracts the viewer's eye, is to:

1. Identify the intent of your message.
2. Employ the four horsemen (see the next section).
3. Match your tone to your meaning.
4. Learn how to navigate silence.
5. Record yourself to learn exactly how you sound.

The Method

Adding color is about making the words you choose stand out and express what you mean more clearly. It's like being on the radio. People can't see you. You have to emphasize words—vary your tone, cadence, and inflection—to express your meaning clearly. Even when people can see you, adding color matters. You have to choose how you're going to emphasize a word or point by selecting one of four categories. As you become a master communicator, this will become second nature. You can become so conscious of how your body responds and how your voice sounds that you no longer have to think about making changes.

The best leaders had to learn this too. You have to use trial and error to find what works for your voice, your body, and your message. The easiest ways to add color are to:

> *Change the speed.* Speak faster or slower to create energy and allow your listeners to follow along.
>
> *Change the volume.* Speak louder or softer to gain their attention.
>
> *Change the stress.* Lengthen or shorten a word to emphasize its meaning.
>
> *Change the inflection.* Raise or lower your pitch to ask a question or assert authority.

These are the four horsemen of delivery. When you pay attention to every one of them, like a jazz musician improvises, you can adapt your speech to engage your listeners. You want them to understand what you're saying without having to work too hard. A listener who has to strain to pay attention to the way you speak doesn't have the cognitive energy to appreciate your message and its meaning.

Even if you get comfortable with the four horsemen, tone matters too. If your tone doesn't match what you're trying to say, people will be confused. If your tone is frustrated and you're trying to tell someone that you believe in her, she simply won't accept it. You may want to be happy for someone, but if your tone doesn't have joy in it, she will think you don't mean it. People won't trust you if your message and your tone aren't consistent.

One more effective way to add color, which grabs people's attention, is to stop talking. Even more powerful, if you are comfortable waiting, is holding the silence like a soufflé that will fall if you're not careful. Holding silence commands the respect of the people in the room. Your ability to pause guarantees that they listen to what you say next. If you lose your train of thought, that's okay. The pause actually helps the listeners prepare for what you're about to say. If you can master silence, you can own the room.

Your ability to add color and highlight it with silence can't improve without help. Again, a trusted colleague, a communication advisor, or the rare spouse who can deliver effective feedback—ideally without reminding you that your real problem is that you left your underwear on the floor (send your spouse Chapter 10 for the proper format for criticizing you)—can make sure that your delivery emphasizes the meaning you intend. Candidates for political office practice for days, sometimes weeks, before debates. Professional speakers do exercises every day to train their voice and master speech. The more time you practice with someone who can give you direct feedback, the more quickly you will know when your speech is most compelling.

QUICK TEST

Are people engaged when you speak? This is not about popularity. If you can add color, you create interest and energy.

The Four Horsemen

Speed

Speed is broken into two parts: rate and pace. Rate is the speed at which your words are put together. Pace is the speed at which your thoughts are put together. You can change the speed of your words to create a dramatic effect, the way a conductor slows or hurries an orchestra. To practice, say, "I am the greatest communicator in the world" as fast as you can. Now say it slowly. Now even more slowly. Now even slower than that. This is not to make you sound ridiculous, although you will. It's to show you the range that you possess right now. You can vary the exact same sentence in intense ways that add incredible energy to what you're saying.

Regarding pace, when you come to a really important point, slow down. You may want to build up a bit of speed before slowly saying the main information that you want people to remember. There is no one right way to change speed. What will become natural for you depends on what your listeners need. If you are speaking to an older crowd, the trend is to go more slowly. Younger listeners usually need more pace. The secret is variation, and the result is that people hang on your words.

Volume

Volume, whether loud or soft, can raise or shrink your ethos. When you can speak in a louder volume, everyone notices. In a big room, this allows you to reach more people. If you're one-on-one or in a meeting, the strategic use of louder volume suggests confidence: you're not afraid to draw attention to what you're saying. If you increase your volume unintentionally, you appear unaware of yourself. If you maintain a loud volume all the time, you become known as the loudmouth.

A whisper can also raise your ethos as a speaker: What you're saying is so special that it's a secret. In a large crowd, you make people feel as if they are among the chosen few who are receiving the inside knowledge. In a group setting, a whisper forces folks to focus in and listen. If this technique is used intentionally and occasionally, your point can be louder with a whisper. If you whisper the whole time, however, you'll be the quiet one on the team.

The best use of volume is within a range. If you are outside this range, people either back away or lean in and ask you to repeat yourself. To know if your volume is normal, the next time you're in a group meeting, place a recorder in the middle of the table and listen to the volume level of the other people in the room compared to your volume when you're talking. Is it easier or more difficult to understand their voices in comparison to yours?

There are two ways to create volume: you can either bang your vocal cords together harder (that's yelling—do it all day and you get a sore throat) or project from your belly. To get louder and not hurt yourself, push out your stomach as you take in a deep breath. This lowers your diaphragm and fills your lungs with more air.

Stress

Changing the stress on a word either stretches the word out or shortens it. It calls attention to a particular word and emphasizes that word's meaning. It shows a sense of confidence that you chose that word on purpose. For instance, if you say that this is a "long" table in a normal voice, your listeners know that you think it's a table of good size. But if you say this is a "loooooooong" table, the emphasis tells them that this is the longest table you have ever seen. You didn't have to say "really, really long," or "This is the longest table ever built." Lengthening a word emphasizes the size or importance of what you're saying.

Inflection

Your inflection is your pitch. It is the raising or lowering of your pitch that either creates a question or asserts your authority. When you ask a question of someone, your pitch goes up at the end of the sentence. In a Western culture, if this happens unintentionally, it's called "uptalk." If your voice goes up at the end of every statement, it sounds as if you are continually asking questions. You come across as tentative. In Asian cultures, uptalk can be a part of the standard pattern of speech, so it is not seen as negative.

If you lower your pitch, you sound powerful. Lower your pitch too far, however, and it can become a distraction. Say the word "yes" in a normal voice. Now say it as a question: "yes?" You've just raised your pitch. Now say it like a giant. When you deepen your pitch, you express a confidence. The key is to be aware of the inflection you are using and why.

Your Tone Is Your Meaning

We start learning about tone at birth. The way a new mother talks to her baby helps us feel comfort. Around the age of two, we learn a different tone, and it doesn't feel good. For example, it's the tone our parents use to yell at us when we are about to touch the hot stove. They say, "Don't touch that." But it's not the words we remember. These experiences of tone stay with us. If you use the wrong tone with your people, you bring up their most primal memories. Their memories interfere with your message.

The best way to learn tone is to practice with someone and record the session. The other person will be able to tell you if you sound like you want to. When you play back your words, you will hear the way you come across. The exercise is simple. Say, "I like cheeseburgers" in different tones. You need to know what you sound like when you are angry, happy, sad, confident, or worried. The secret with tone is that the meaning is independent of the words. When you know how to add the right tone to match what you're saying, your message becomes clear.

A common example of this is "I'm gonna kill you." If it's someone saying this to his brother, he may just be angry. If someone is saying this to her best friend who did something nice, the tone suggests that she shouldn't have. If it's a dangerous criminal saying it, the tone probably means real trouble. Tone portrays meaning and needs as much attention as the words you choose.

How to Win an Election: George Bush and Barack Obama

George Bush was repeatedly captured bumbling his words and saying the wrong thing during his runs for president and time in office. But he still was more compelling than John Kerry on the campaign trail. John Kerry's speeches were like a white wall, where nothing was clear because everything sounded the same. While Kerry was able to break his speech pattern and sound more conversational when he talked about his family, George Bush won the election because he used a tone that more people could connect with when talking politics.

Barack Obama was not a proven leader when he was elected in 2008, but he was a proven speaker. John McCain had the experience. He was a war hero. But on the campaign trail, no matter how good his ideas were, he often sounded angry. Hundreds of people came out to see John McCain. Tens of thousands came to hear Barack Obama. There was no crowd that he could not rally, and no speech that he could not infuse with a charisma that people remembered. His tone further emphasized his message. People didn't have to work to get the feeling of his vision. They may not have even remembered what he said, but they wanted to follow.

This lesson is not only political. It's about the power of communication. If you cannot strategically change your tone so that it matches your intended message, the person who can will beat you even if your ideas are better. She will close the deal, she will get the promotion, and she will be the leader that people want to follow.

They Will Sit on the Edge of Their Seats

Just listen. Wherever you are, listen. What do you notice? The simple act of intentionally listening heightens your sensitivity to sound. When you pause in any communication, you are doing the same thing. Pauses are comforting in a presentation because they allow your listeners a brief moment to catch up. If your pauses are too predictable, however, your speech will develop a repetitious pattern. That will lull your listeners into a trance or lead them to imagine going to the beach.

With a big crowd, before you start, pause. In between stories, pause. Before a transition, pause. Before you are about to tell your audience the most important thing they have ever heard another human being utter, pause for a long time and look beyond the crowd. You have just colored your next words with gold.

Say, "Silence reveals the message."
- Now count to one in your head in between each word.
- Now count to two after saying "Silence," then finish the sentence.
- Now count to three after saying "Silence reveals" before saying "the message."

What did it feel like to pause? It may be uncomfortable at first. When you can trust yourself enough to intentionally be quiet in conversations, meetings, or presentations, you can command attention.

The Pros

Professional speakers, whether on the lecture circuit or in the media, add notes to their presentations to remind them where to add color. You might never see this because the speakers have completely mastered their talk. But they went through an intentional process to master the four horsemen, tone, and pausing.

They begin by underlining the words where they want to add impact. Many of them usually work in pencil because as they practice, they figure out what's really at the core of their message. Then they test whether to add volume or stress, speed or inflection. In addition to underlining, they use arrows up and down for volume or inflection. They will add a slash at any place they want to pause, adding extra slashes for additional seconds.

With a marked-up script, they record themselves. Even the pros record themselves or work with communication coaches. Even if you have become one of the best speakers in the world, no two talks are exactly the same. Every group of listeners needs a different emphasis to understand what you're really trying to make clear. For those who present without a script, the effort is the same, but they write down color words as a list. The list reminds them not only of their message, but of the intentional moments where they need to employ the four horsemen.

Rarely in your working life will you have to use a teleprompter. Most executives run into them only at big conferences, during a video

recording for investors, or when doing a webinar. Teleprompters introduce another person into your presentation, controlling the speed at
which the text will flow across the screen. It is essential that you practice with that person ahead of time or describe the way you like to talk.
Pros always check in with the teleprompter operator because that quick
relationship can determine how effective you'll be in a high-pressure
situation. Free software that simulates using a teleprompter is available
for any computer if you need to practice.

How to Sound Like a Leader

Cultural Color

An American speaks in a loud, direct voice. If the volume is louder than
normal, an American audience knows that the speaker is extremely
serious about what he is saying. But for many Indian men, this is how
they talk when they are comfortable. Now suppose an Indian man is
speaking with a Malaysian woman. He thinks he's being friendly when
he speaks in a loud, direct voice. She thinks he's being rude. The color
you use depends on whom you are talking to and where you are. Take
the time to learn the cultural norms of speakers for the location where
you plan to present.

How Cold Is Your Water?

You may not have time to exercise your voice, but you can make sure
that you don't damage it. You already know that you shouldn't drink
caffeine, alcohol, or dairy products before a talk because they change
your voice. What is the biggest secret to sounding great? Room-
temperature water. Your vocal cords are muscles. Chill the muscle and
you lose the flexibility. You will lose the dynamic quality of the voice
that you already have if your vocal cords are cold. Room-temperature
water keeps your voice lubricated, and the words will sound better.

Plosive Sounds and Assimilation

Assimilation is the blending of sounds, blurring the listener's understanding of what you are saying. When you say "Gimme" instead of

"Give me" or "Ya wanna" instead of "You want to," you can sound sloppy. Assimilating words is not a big deal by itself. If you say, "Gimme a cup of water," around people who know your speech pattern, you'll probably get a cup of water. But once you're around people who don't know the way you speak, if you assimilate, you could be misunderstood or seen as too casual.

The reason has to do with our brain's amazing ability to process information. The average person talks at about 183 words per minute. You can think at about 600 words per minute. That means that the average person has around 400 words a minute bouncing around in his head while you're talking. He can spend that bandwidth either processing your message and reacting to it or struggling to pay attention. Assimilating forces your listener to work harder. That's why listening to someone with an unfamiliar accent exhausts you.

Everyone assimilates. Even sign language has versions of assimilation. Master communicators can turn it off in a second by emphasizing plosive sounds. In the English language there are dozens of phonemes, the units that make up the plosives. The exact number varies between dialects and countries. This is not a lesson in speech therapy, but be aware that eight specific sounds make up the plosives. If you don't emphasize these sounds, your words get lost. You need to know these sounds so people hear your most important messages if you want to come across as a leader.

B as in *boy*	J as in *jump*	K as in *kite*
D as in *dog*	P as in *Peter*	Ch as in *chocolate*
G as in *girl*	T as in *toy*	

The sounds are called plosives because they explode out of your mouth. When you assimilate, you implode the sounds. Instead of saying, "Don't," you drop the *t* off. Other people hear "Don." Most listeners are polite enough to fill in the *t* for you. But you're making your listeners do the work. That doesn't mean that you should walk around hitting every single plosive all the time.

There are three situations where you definitely want to hit them. The first is any time you're on the telephone, where your listeners do not have nonverbal communication to help them. Second, you use them any time you use technical terms. A technical term is any term that your listener doesn't know. Even your name is a technical term if your listener doesn't know it. Third, you use them any time you want to sound authoritative. If you turn on the plosive sounds, you will see an immediate reaction.

When you start hitting strategic plosives, you'll notice a difference in your listeners' response. Try delivering the frame for a meeting, the one-sentence summary of what you need your team to get done right away. Simply telling someone he did a "GreaT JoB!" emphasizes the validation. Plosives break you out of your speech pattern and reveal your confidence in your message. When you start using them more often, no one will approach you and say, "Hey, nice plosives!" People will simply feel that you mean what you're saying, and that you're not afraid to emphasize that it's important. Assimilation isn't wrong. The skill is to be able to turn it on or off.

PRACTICE THE TECHNIQUE

Drill 1: Playing with Tone

With your team, practice tone like your next deal depends on it.

1. Pick a sentence that relates to your company—a mantra or tagline. For example, if you worked for Nike, "Just Do It."
2. Have someone pick a tone, such as angry, happy, or mean.
3. Have the group pick someone to say the phrase in that tone.
4. Have the person do it until the group finds the tone believable.
5. Have that same person pick another tone and pick the next person.
6. Repeat until everyone has had a turn.

This kind of improvisational drill with your team may feel artificial at first. Some people may find it to be uncomfortable. But the payoff will be worth it when they can control their tone in front of clients and other listeners.

Drill 2: Counting to Three

Before making the most important point of your presentation, count to three. Watch the eyes in the room as they suddenly all look at you expectantly.

1. Know the point you want everyone to remember.
2. Be silent for three seconds right before you deliver that point.

Be sure it is your most important point, because your listeners will remember what you say next.

Drill 3: Overexploding

If you practice the plosives enough, they will become natural.

1. Say, "Plosives are neat but hard to repeat" five times.
2. Emphasize the plosives—words with *B, D, G, J, P, T, K,* and *CH.*
3. Record yourself.
4. Circle the sounds you dropped.
5. Emphasize them and say it faster.

The more quickly you can say the sentence, emphasizing every plosive, the more natural the sounds will feel to your listener, and the more he will be engaged in your communication.

THE TEST

How hard do people have to work to understand what you're saying? When you add color, the room changes. Faces light up. People's body language is more engaged. They are more interested in what you have to say because they don't have to struggle to understand you. The more people have to process what you mean, the less time they have to consider whether they agree with your message. The less you make them work, the more they can focus on solving problems and figuring out the next great thing.

THE MOMENTS THAT NEED YOUR LEADERSHIP

A Brief Introduction to Section 2

In a research study of 468 groups from diverse organizations around the world, we asked a simple question: "What builds strong relationships?" Over 70 percent of the participants used the same two words: *trust* and *communication*. The question is: How? How do you communicate in the difficult moments, like overcoming defensiveness or delivering feedback?

The answer: Master specific formats for effective communication. The more interconnected, virtual, and unpredictable our world becomes, the more ways you have to communicate and the more challenging it is to lead your team toward what they need to do. Too many things change too quickly. They go wrong in an instant. These are the moments that need you.

The formats in the following chapters will help you prepare and deliver effective communication for the most difficult moments at work. These are proven formulas for how to plan what you're going to say and say it well. Whether you are new to leadership or a seasoned leader, you will continue to face these predictable situations. Your ability to rise and succeed will depend on your performance in the six moments. You can always be ready with a playbook to connect and build trust.

CHAPTER 7

DEFENSIVENESS

Defensiveness prevents clear communication. The reaction happens because a person feels threatened. Whether the causes are from inside or outside of an organization, defensiveness presents as rigid, stuck communication. In this chapter, you will learn how to recognize your own defensiveness and how to defuse it in others.

The First Moment: Defensiveness

If your listeners are defensive, your message will most likely be lost. Something has caused them to feel that you, whether intentionally or not, are attacking them or their idea. This emotion causes them to focus on defending their content or character instead of exploring solutions. They are struggling, and it may be your fault.

You may not have set the right expectations. You may have used a tone that didn't match your intended message. You may not have given them the resources to achieve their goals. They may just be tired. If you engage their defensiveness, you will make it worse. If you know how to approach their defensiveness, you can instantly redirect their negative energy—whether it's fear, doubt, or worry—and help them leave the conversation with your message.

The Trap

They say no. You say yes. They say, "I didn't know." You say, "You should have." Maybe you were taught to ask questions as a way of managing effectively, so you say, "How could you not know?" But this question suggests that they are somehow not smart because they did not know. While that may not be your intended message, it's there. Their spines will rise and their eyes will narrow. If you react to their posturing instead of listening and helping them to sit back and reflect on what's bothering them, they will react as well. Instead of focusing on the real purpose of your conversation, they will fight you.

If you are in a conversation and you notice that someone is getting defensive, stop. Don't go any further with your point. Don't try to make your point in a different way. This will rarely work. If someone is defensive, he isn't listening. He has one agenda, and that is to deflect what he thinks is your attack. You may need to just listen to ask a question like "What do you need?" or to say, "Help me understand your point of view." Then stop. You may have to continue the conversation at another time. The fact that you take the time to process and digest that conversation is validation. That's the first step in overcoming defensiveness.

You can fall into this trap even when you go into a conversation knowing that someone might be defensive. If you haven't prepared how you want to approach her emotion, rigid belief, or confusion, she will stay shut down and retreat deeper into herself. To help her come to a decision or understand your point of view without feeling defensive, the format to use is called "defensive persuasion."

The Format

1. *Validate first.* If people are to be comfortable, they have to know that you value their opinion on whatever issue is causing their defensiveness even if you disagree. Decide how you're going to validate. Will it be a head nod? Listening? Paraphrasing? (See Chapter 5.) People can't open their minds until they know you have heard and understood their

point—especially when you completely disagree with it. Even in established relationships, you will need to validate. You won't need to do this as often, but if people are fired up, the only way to cool them down is to show them that you recognize their value or the value of their contribution.

2. *Frame.* What message do you want them to get? You have to decide this ahead of time. (See Chapter 4). That's why if you run into someone who is defensive and you can't figure out why and he won't tell you, you have to end the current conversation. If you don't know the message you want the person to understand, the conversation will go in circles. He will stay defensive.

3. *Decide your timeline.* You may not overcome someone's emotion in one conversation. In fact, it may take many. Sometimes you will have to validate for two or three conversations before you can frame what you need from the other person. If you have done this well, the trust you build will allow you to communicate more immediately the next time.

The Queen of Hearts: How It Works

Defensive persuasion is about helping someone come to a conclusion without feeling defensive. It's about knowing that human beings get stuck for all kinds of reasons. As a leader or manager, if you want to take advantage of someone's talent, you may not be able to communicate in the way that is most comfortable for you. Learning defensive persuasion is not magic. Navigating the format, however, is easiest with a deck of cards.

Try this exercise with a friend. From a traditional deck of playing cards, write down a specific card—for example, the queen of hearts. Turn the paper over, and don't show it to your friend. Explain that you're going to teach her defensive persuasion, and that you wrote down the name of a card on a piece of paper so that she can see how this technique works. The reason you tell her this out loud is so that she doesn't think this is a trick. You've just framed the exercise.

Continue by asking your friend if she is familiar with a deck of cards. Of course she will be, and she has just gotten a question right. You've just validated her knowledge. As minor a validation as this may sound, the impact of every affirmation in a relationship creates trust.

Even if she answers, "Not really," don't judge her. Say, "No problem," and introduce the deck in a helpful tone of voice. Then keep going.

Ask, "How many suits are in a deck of cards?"

She will answer, "Four." You say, "Great."

Then you ask, "What are those four suits?" She will say, "Clubs, spades, hearts, and diamonds," or something similar. You say, "Great."

Ask her what the colors are in a deck of cards. She will say, "Black and red."

So far, you helped your friend feel comfortable and allowed her to show off what she knows. Here's where you shift from asking questions with answers she knows to the validating and framing that make defensive persuasion so powerful.

Ask her to choose a color. Remember, your card is the queen of hearts. You don't even need her to say, "Red."

If she says, "Red," you say, "Great," and keep going. If she says, "Black," you say "Great, and that leaves us with the red," and keep going.

The entire strategy is based on your ability to validate in the moment. You wouldn't say, "Greeeat!" as you would if she closed a major deal, or "GRRReat," as if you wish she'd never said that. The tone of your voice will tell the person whether you've validated her or judged her. You say, "Great," with a balanced tone, as if you're saying hello to a colleague and you're happy to see her.

When you then start talking about the red card, your friend will come with you. If you do it in a positive way, she'll come with you to talk about the red cards even though she selected black. If she pushes back hard and stops you to say, "But I said black," go with her. Say, "I like the black cards too. I loved playing spades as a kid." Take a few moments to talk about the black cards. Then bring the discussion back to red. Listeners aren't defensive when you validate their answers.

Even though she picked the wrong card, emotionally, you let her know that this wasn't a problem. If you don't validate her, she won't be able to get past the fact that you're not talking about the black cards.

She will listen out of politeness, but she will either stop you or stop paying attention. Because she has become defensive, the conversation is over.

As you talk about the red cards—say, "Which suits make up the red cards?"—this lets your friend show off minor knowledge again.

She will answer, "Diamonds and hearts." Say, "Great."

Ask her to choose one of those.

If she chooses hearts, say, "Great," and keep going. If she chooses diamonds, say, "Great. That leaves us with the hearts," and keep going.

Now explain that we can break all the hearts into two groups, face cards and number cards. Ask her to pick a group. Make sure to ask her for a group, not a card.

If she says, "Face cards," say, "Great," and keep going. If she says, "Number cards," say, "Great. That leaves us with the face cards." This exercise is to emphasize that you can always validate and you can always direct a conversation in a specific direction.

Now ask her to tell you what the face cards are. If she includes the ace, don't debate her—just go with it. *The key to defensive persuasion is to know where you are taking the person, and not to worry about being right or wrong.* Communication as a leader is not about being the smartest person or the person with all the answers. Your opportunity is to make sure that everyone understands what they need to do to be successful.

Once your friend answers jack, queen, and king, ask her to pick one of those.

If she says, "Queen," say "Great, that's the card I chose," and you're done. If she says, "Jack," say, "Great. That leaves us with what?" Let *her* tell you what's left. Pause for a moment. Look at how far you've gone in this conversation. You went from 52 cards down to 2: the queen and the king of hearts. When she says, "Queen and king," ask her to choose one of those. If she chooses the queen, say, "Great, that was my card." If she chooses the king, say, "Great," and ask her what's left.

When she says, "Queen," say, "Great," then flip over the piece of paper.

This way of learning defensive persuasion exposes the key principles of the format. Defensive persuasion won't work without validation.

In the deck of cards example, you're using the word *great* as the validator. The exercise takes about a minute. If you're good at it, it can be entertainment at lunch or drinks to start a conversation with colleagues about how the group communicates.

In real defensive moments, the validator will vary according to the person and the situation. But the more regularly you validate the value of your colleagues, the easier it is for them to hear the core messages that you want them to embrace.

The amount of time required for a real-world transformation varies. It could be short. It could take days. When you're improving a teammate's performance, it could take a quarter or longer. You need to develop your timeline as you strategize. Sticking with the deck of cards, for example, on Monday, you ask the person to pick a color. Because you know that this person is really defensive, you stop there. He has just picked a color. You say, "Great," and walk away. You won't ask the next question until the next day. You space out the validations and the questions so the person can know you value him.

And master communicators definitely define where they want people to go ahead of time. The validations and frames of defensive persuasion do not always happen off the top of your head. In fact, few people can do that. Sales professionals often can because they are familiar with selling a single product all the time. For most people, however, taking the time to write your validations and frames down ahead of time is the secret to becoming good at it.

How to Work with Rivals: Abraham Lincoln

When Abraham Lincoln dealt with defensive, angry people, he waited. Then he validated in creative ways because he knew where the country needed to go. His preparation and method changed America forever. In Doris Kearns Goodwin's book *Team of Rivals: The Political Genius of Abraham Lincoln*, she traces Lincoln's leadership acumen from the perspective of others. Using the writings of those closest to him, she discovered how he led the United States through one of its darkest periods.

Lincoln didn't fall for defensiveness. He had conversations based on the long-run goals of the nation. Those goals were the frame at the center of every conversation. They were where he wanted to take people in each interaction. He rarely let personal feelings distract him. As Goodwin told us in our interview with her:

> What was so terrific about Lincoln is that instead of allowing himself to be upset with someone else who was jockeying around or even saying hurtful things to him, instead of getting his back up and becoming defensive, he could somehow try and see the situation from the other person's point of view. He sought to understand where they were coming from. He knew that in the long run if he could get that person to work in a positive way with him he could forget these slights and make it possible for both of them to come out better.

Lincoln was a master validator, and his favorite method was humor. "The great thing about humor, especially when it is self-deprecating humor, is it allows people to become part of that moment instead of attacking you," says Goodwin. "Somebody yelled at him, 'Lincoln, you're two-faced.' And he turns around and says, 'If I had two faces, do you think I'd be wearing this face?'"

If humor is not natural for you, choose another validator. Like Lincoln did, explore the other person's point of view. Paraphrase it back to the person. Show them you appreciate their opinion even if you don't agree. "That takes a certain kind of perspective," admits Goodwin. "Instead of responding immediately when something needs to be dealt with, you think about it. Waiting to respond is, in fact, a validator. It shows the other person their argument is worth your time."

When you are defensive, wait as well. "That great ritual he had, instead of angrily getting upset with someone when something went wrong. He had the tendency to write what he called 'hot letters.' He got all of his emotions down in the letter and then put it aside hoping he could cool down psychologically. Then he never needed to send it." For you as a leader or manager, apply Lincoln's technique by writing the heated email, but not sending it.

When you do have to express strong emotion, Lincoln is still the role model. "When he did finally get angry with people, he would follow up with a kind gesture. How wonderful it must have been if you'd had a bad time in a discussion with him and then you go back to your office and there's a handwritten letter saying, 'If I did get up in anger, I don't have sufficient time to keep it up.' And then it's over. Those bad feelings don't fester." Lincoln was consistently validating and then directing people to a vision of a better world. You can be the same kind of leader if your frames are clear and you believe validation matters.

Unhook Your Attitude

The people you work with have attitudes. An attitude is a fixed thought, general feeling, or belief. Attitudes become opinions, and you and the other members of your team have opinions about everything. They may not be saying what they think, but they have a position. When two opinions clash, the result is defensiveness. You can instantly make the situation better or worse in a word. You can literally flip someone's whole day and his ability to be effective in the near term if you can unhook *your* attitude.

Your attitude becomes communication. The way you think about something will dictate your tone. We categorize attitude in two ways: personal attitudes and professional attitudes. When you're using your professional attitude, you know how to communicate well. However, once you've been "hooked," you get pulled into your personal attitudes, and you're no longer communicating about your work. Rather, you're giving your personal thoughts on the topic or situation. The skill is to unhook, as Lincoln did. To unhook your attitude is to clean the chalkboard of your mind.

As a leader or manager, how you deal with your attitudes and the attitudes of your team members will determine your ability to communicate. The moment you unhook, the wrinkles in your face actually flatten. The fire in your eyes calms. The other person who is defensive is no longer a threat to you. And there's one more small benefit. You'll think clearly again.

When you are unhooked, using any of the techniques and applying the format is easier. If your listener initially stays defensive, you're not worried about it. You know you will be able to defuse the person eventually. He will see you listen. You will become a force for good in his life. Now you can apply the format because you are not trying to win a war. Once again you are partnering so that you can achieve together. As a side note, even the masters get hooked. The difference is that the masters choose to unhook more often or remove themselves from the situation until they can take a step back and communicate effectively.

Attitudes come from every experience you've ever had and every place you've ever been. If you're unaware of your attitudes, they will bite you. Attitudes can be barriers if you don't know they are there. Your teammates' attitudes are rarely shallow. If you are unaware of their positions on what's important in your work and in their life, you will create pain in your relationship that was entirely avoidable. When you unhook, you can help them let go too. Hooked communicators struggle to get people to the queen of hearts.

When You Know People Are Going to Be Defensive

You Need Them to Work Late

The members of your team will need to stay late, maybe until ten o'clock, to prepare all the equipment that has to be shipped off to the trade show. If you come in Monday morning and say, "Tom, I need you to stay until 10," you know how he's going to react.

Instead you say, "Hey, Tom, have everyone meet me in the warehouse because we have to get this stuff shipped out today." You've said nothing about staying late and you've set the initial frame.

When everyone meets you there, you say, "There's lots to do. What has to get done today?" You've still said nothing about staying late, and you've immediately validated your team members' ability to figure out what it takes to do the work right. Once they've figured out the needs, you say, "So who's taking responsibility for what?" There's still nothing about staying late. If some people don't want to own part of the project, say, "I need everyone to take one part of the project to make sure it gets done right. Who wants which role?"

Once the roles are divided, you say, "This needs to get done so that it can go out first thing tomorrow morning." Your team members know their jobs and the timeline, and you've said nothing about staying late.

But if one of your teammates is skilled at avoiding work, he may say in the middle, "I can't stay late today, and I know we can't get this done before five." Remember the format: validate first, and then focus on your queen of hearts.

You say, "Great, so what do we need to do to get this out tomorrow morning?" Instead of saying, "You have to stay," you've put the burden of how the work will get done on him. In front of all his teammates, either the person has to step up or you will be having a different kind of conversation (more on feedback in Chapter 10).

Remember, defensive persuasion does not mean that people will do whatever you say. It minimizes or eliminates the defensiveness. In most cases, the person ultimately will agree to work late. At the very least, you'll be able to have a direction conversation without the defensive attitude, thus strengthening the overall relationship.

Your Whole Organization Is Defensive

You're the leader of 300 people. You don't have time to sit down with every single person and clarify why you're cutting budgets. Your people know that business has been slow, but they have gotten used to a certain way of doing things and they don't like the changes.

You make the right first move and create a feedback forum for your top leadership. You gather the group of 30. You feed everyone. Well-fed lions rarely eat their trainers. You open with a quick statement about knowing how difficult the changes are for their teams and that you want all their ideas about how to improve the situation. The first comment comes from one of your better leaders. He says, "I really think we should consider going organic on our daily lunch buffets."

You can't believe what you've just heard. You're dealing with million-dollar problems. This person, who is supposed to be a senior executive, asks about the free lunch—which may not be here too much longer if business doesn't pick up. The comment is definitely out of place, but what you say next decides whether anyone else is going to talk.

You say, paying attention to your tone, "Tell me more. What would you like to see?" After another comment on the importance of healthy eating for keeping the company healthy, you say, "I love that you're thinking broadly about the health of our team. We'll look into that." Then you can redirect the conversation back to the immediate topic.

Because you validated this question, four other hands shoot up. You have just taught everyone in the room that it is safe to speak in this environment. The way you handle every comment, even when it's out of place, decides whether the environment is safe for people to say what they really think. You didn't condescend to the questioner, and you didn't agree either.

When people are defensive as you walk into the room, they're thinking, "Here's management ready to shove crap down my throat." You have to be calm and approachable. You have to show them that you value what they offer, even when it's not very helpful. That way they will understand and buy into the direction you need them to move.

An Angry Room

Defusing anger is all about listening as validation. You will need to prove that you hear people, understand their message, and value their participation. Normally, you don't just say, "Thank you. I value your participation," because it may come out as insincere. You may need to be creative in how you listen.

For instance, have the person that everyone in the organization is comfortable talking with walk around to capture comments about senior management. Then get everyone in a room and, one by one, flash the comments, anonymously but in raw form. Don't be afraid of the negative comments. It takes intention and courage to show that you want to get better. Open by saying "So, guys, we've been listening to you, and here's what we've heard."

If you gathered the real pain that people are feeling and you post it—ideas like "The senior management in this company doesn't communicate strategy well"—it is honest and powerful. You have just shown people that you hear what they are saying. What you do next is very important. You either answer the criticism or acknowledge that you don't know the answer, but you see it as a priority.

If your situation allows for humor, you could say something playful like "Well, we've gotta fix that." Your response is loose because you can't believe the reality is this bad. Variations with a playful tone like "Well, that's not good" can show people you see the need for change. At a certain point, you will need to offer solutions. But the humor and pointing to what can be different through the slides can switch anger into openness.

One-on-One

Someone storms into your office saying that his coworker stole his project. You know that he is motivated by power, so this is a big deal for him. The simple way to validate and then frame is to say, "Feel, felt, found." For example: "Steve, I can see that you *feel* frustrated by this whole thing. If I had been in your shoes, I would have *felt* the same way. What I have *found* is . . ."

Listening to the initial burst of frustration, describing what you observe the person feeling, and stating that you would have felt the same way validates his emotion. Most managers just start with *found* and tell the person the fix. In the case of the stolen project, they will say, "Go talk to him." That is the solution, but if the person is defensive, he's not ready for the queen of hearts yet.

If you're a manager and someone comes barging into your office upset, your job is to listen, give good eye contact, and demonstrate that you are paying attention. In your mind, control your attitude. You may not have time for this. But if you don't validate him, he will leave your office frustrated and distracted from his work. His productivity will go down. Give him five minutes and you save five days or five months of his time.

This doesn't mean that you have to listen all day. At a certain point, when the person either starts to repeat himself, slows down the speed of his voice, or pauses long enough to show you that he is done, say, "This is really helpful to me to hear what's going on." Or you can say, "Help me make sure I've got the experience right." Then repeat back to him what you heard in your own words.

Then you can give an actual answer—what you've *found* to work in the past. If you don't know the answer, don't bluff. Say, "This is helpful. Let me think about it, and we'll talk again tomorrow." That will be enough if you successfully validate, and you can deliver the "feel, felt, found" format in the next conversation.

How Do You Know the Format Worked?

You know people are no longer defensive when their demeanor changes. Watch their eye contact and body language. If they are defensive, they can't look you in the eye. They will be either extremely aggressive or completely withdrawn. When you've validated them, they relax. The tone of their voice becomes less penetrating. At the end of the day, not only are they more likely to do what you suggest, but they may even pop their head in and say, "Thank you." They are grateful that you heard them, even if you didn't agree with them.

After you validate people, if they've really heard your message, they can paraphrase your frame, if not use your exact words. When you ask them to explain the importance of your conversation, they have a new attitude. They have a clear position about the value of the work you're doing or the behavior you're asking them to embrace. To get this sign of their reengagement, before a conversation ends, say, "Let's spend five minutes making sure we've heard each other." Then you can ask, "What are our takeaways from this conversation?" If they didn't hear you, they will say, a little embarrassed, "I guess I don't know." In this case, clarify what you meant. Use the opportunity to reaffirm they don't need to be defensive around you in the future.

CHAPTER 8

MEETINGS

Meetings happen one-on-one, in small groups, and as an entire organization. When a meeting is poorly run, people lose focus. They feel their time is wasted. In this chapter, you will learn how to organize memorable, efficient meetings that maximize the potential of your time together.

The Second Moment: Meetings

Harena in Latin means "sand." In ancient Rome, it was the center of an amphitheater where the gladiators battled. When we think of an arena today, we imagine rock stars, political rallies, and championship games. In the Roman Empire, the arena was not the stands or the grand coliseum of stone and mortar. It was the sand that soaked up the blood of defeat. At the end of a battle, all you had to do to start over was throw sand, and the arena was new. Remove the violence, and the metaphor is beautiful.

What if you had spaces at work where you could debate, brainstorm, and challenge the way things happen? What if your meetings could embrace the conflict that is normal when teammates battle to figure out what is best? What if you knew each day where to go to truly connect to the people with whom you work? The difference in organizations that innovate and manage change gracefully is that they are experts at "meeting."

The Trap

A poor setup is the trap, and it creates an even bigger sinkhole: reverting to stress communication tendencies. The inductive communicators will struggle to get to the point. The deductive communicators will state their ideas with the point first as if it is the end of the conversation. In Chapter 2, we talked about internal and external communication. The amount of silence that someone needs before responding to something you say determines whether the person is an internal communicator (someone who thinks before speaking) or an external communicator (someone who thinks out loud).

When a meeting lacks fundamental structure, the externals start talking and don't stop. They are trying to figure out how to be valuable, and they do that with words the way Jackson Pollack threw paint at a canvas. Internals don't talk. They have great ideas, but because the meeting lacks clarity, they keep their thoughts to themselves. Just creating an arena is not enough to foster the right kind of comfort to allow participants to think clearly and share ideas freely. Great meetings begin with articulate, pointed setups.

The Format

If you are just getting together with someone casually for drinks and talking about work or doing a preliminary interview or exploration of a project you might do together, this format isn't necessary. This format is for internal meetings at work, both live and virtual. This is how, as a leader or manager, you can stop wasting time. As more of us work longer and harder than ever before, this format is how you make sure meeting time is wisely spent.

1. *Have someone facilitate.* A meeting without a facilitator is like a war without a general. The troops will run around without a clear focus, and they will eventually panic and retreat. The facilitator either takes the agenda or makes the agenda. He facilitates the conversation so that tension

doesn't become war, the meeting stays on an intentional track, and everyone leaves with a clear resolution about what to do next. The facilitator validates participants. The facilitator paraphrases salient points. Even if it's a standing meeting, someone has to intentionally announce, "I'll be facilitating (or leading) today's meeting," or name another teammate as the leader: "I'd like Rick to run the meeting today."

In virtual meetings, the facilitator's role is the same, but exaggerated. Where you can read the body language in person, faces are often blank virtually. That doesn't mean someone isn't paying attention. It does mean, when you don't see heads nodding, you have to ask for confirmation that someone agrees or disagrees with an idea. You may need to ask people to put their hands up to show their opinions on a solution. The facilitator is not just keeping the agenda and focus in the virtual world. The job is to confirm engagement because everyone experiences extra distractions when working remotely.

2. *Set the time frame.* The leader or facilitator then sets the time frame. In most cases, this will be done in advance. Pick a time frame both for the entire meeting and often for each topic on the agenda. In many meetings, it's a good idea to spend the first few minutes confirming the agenda and how long should be spent on each topic. This way, as things change, the facilitator can gauge how long to let one topic go over or cut another to keep the overall meeting time on track. One thing we've seen for certain is that people tend to be very forgiving when meetings end early, but not so much when they run over without permission. So, if you know the time frame, and you see that the meeting is going to go long, as the facilitator, you need to check in with the group to ensure that the meeting priorities are met.

3. *Clarify the purpose.* There is a hook to the meeting that you're about to have. Take a moment to clarify and create a one-sentence reason for the time you're spending together.

Can't do it? Take a few minutes by yourself or with a trusted advisor to figure it out. Consider how you frame that statement to keep everyone focused. It could be as simple as "Today we are meeting to decide our marketing budget for next quarter." If the room is filled with inductive thinkers, add a few details after the purpose and restate the reason for gathering at the end. You can be inductive and still be brief.

4. *Set the ground rules for the conversation.* In some cultures, these do not need to be spelled out. For example, if a company has a specific format for solving problems, everyone may already be familiar with how a meeting flows. If not, teach your teammates ahead of time (especially new members of your team).

5. *Determine the type of conversation.* If the facilitator is not explicit, someone will be venting when everyone else is trying to make a decision, and you will lose focus. More on this in the next section.

6. *Agree on the next steps.* Those attending the meeting may have heard mixed messages, or the meeting may have covered lots of things. To make sure everyone knows what she's responsible for, say, "Before we end, let's talk about what the next steps are," or "What did we just agree to?" By closing with "Let's spend a few minutes summarizing what we just discussed," you make sure that the group is in agreement and people know what they own going forward.

Choose the Type of Conversation

Making sure that everyone knows the type of conversation you're about to have prevents frustration and the wrong kind of conflict. The way you want people to approach communication in a meeting is just as important as what you're talking about. There are as many kinds of meetings as your creativity can envision. These are the common forms. When you name the type of meeting at the beginning, this has an unanticipated power to focus your team.

Debate. Deliberating, arguing, and sometimes challenging each other's ideas. This type of conversation often fosters conflict, and this is good because it's intentional. But here's the key: the debate has to be about the ideas. The moment debate gets personal, people leave feeling disrespected and demotivated. For a healthy debate, the facilitator needs to keep the discussion on the ideas, not personal attacks.

Brainstorming. Freely throwing out ideas without debating their value or coming to a conclusion. Never forget about the internal communicators. They will usually be the last to speak, or they will not speak at all, but they have been processing during the whole meeting. They may have the best ideas and need to be invited to offer them. A strong facilitator invites every voice to participate and validates all the ideas. This public validation even of ideas that don't have merit will encourage the less confident participants to speak up. There are no "right or wrong, good or bad" ideas when brainstorming. Don't worry if you hear an idea that you think is crazy or off-topic. Let it out. Brainstorming is about squeezing the creative juices, and you can refine them later.

Informational. Offering something that you know to be true without debating or brainstorming or coming to a conclusion. Be prepared, add color, and see Chapter 11 for how to master a meeting presentation. People will start playing on their phones the moment you aren't engaging.

Venting. Sharing your feelings about what's happened without judging those feelings, debating, brainstorming, or offering other information. This is not therapy, but it is sometimes essential to just let people say what they feel. Your job is not to fix the feelings, only to validate them—to value that people have shared the things that really bother them. Then, reframe the conversation to focus on what's most important now.

Decision making. Reaching a conclusion. This is one of the rarest and most precious moments in every arena and any organization.

When you get good at framing a meeting, you don't just say, "We'll meet for 30 minutes." You say, "After a few minutes of venting about last quarter's results, let's brainstorm a new strategy and spend the last five minutes deciding our new direction." If you don't set the clear focus of the meeting and then clarify how you want your team to explore that focus, you will get each person having a different kind of meeting at the same time.

If one person is venting and another person is trying to make a decision, both people will leave frustrated. That can end their effectiveness for the day. The externals will seek out anyone who will listen to tell him what a horrible meeting they just experienced and how clearly everything is falling apart. The internals will simply stop talking, to anyone. Whatever the arena, this step in the format prevents drama and promotes focus.

To Agenda or Not to Agenda

Every formal meeting needs an agenda. Participants need the purpose of the meeting, the subsequent topics, and the timelines sent in an email to everyone ahead of the gathering. Ideally, the facilitator checks the agenda's direction with a few leaders before the meeting to make sure people are prepared. The agenda should be on a screen in the room, or as hard copies for in-person meetings, as the meeting starts. For virtual meetings, attach it to the platform's file-sharing function, post it in the chat, or share your screen for a few minutes while doing the initial framing. Agendas do not need to be overly detailed or complicated.

Not every meeting, however, needs a written agenda. If your organization uses Agile methodology for project management, stand-ups have a regular pattern. They have a consistent agenda, and the scrum master—the facilitator in Agile—notes any changes before the meeting begins. One-to-one or small group casual meetings, whether regular or one-time, may not need a written outline ahead of time either. They do still need clarity at the beginning of the conversation about why each person is there.

Even for casual meetings, however, turn the agreed-upon topics into a follow-up email after the meeting. In formal meetings, always have the note-keeper or facilitator send out the results of the meeting. When people are busy, it is easy to let agreements slip because they weren't documented. The same is true with causal meetings. Agree at the end who will document the conclusions. If you are the junior member of the meeting or the person who wants to rise, sending the follow-up email shows you are attentive and communicate intentionally. Leaders will remember your effort.

The Silent Types and the Loudmouths

Translation: some people won't talk, and other people can't stop. As a leader running a meeting, pay attention to each participant's tendency before the meeting. Internal thinkers need at least a little time, and sometimes days, before they can truly express out loud what they think. This is not a character flaw, although you might think so if your tendency is different. This is their nature. Whether they learned it from their family, it's a yet-undiscovered genomic trait, or that's the way the successful people they've watched communicate, they need time to process information before they speak.

The other category in this ancient duality is the talkers. External thinkers have no filter. They may want to have a filter, but if they get an idea, they have to speak it. You say something, and they will say something back. They have an opinion on everything. Of course, external thinkers can learn to have a filter. It's hard for them, and if they are under stress, they may revert to old tendencies. They are usually not trying to take over the meeting. They actually need to process everything out loud.

Of course, the talkers can derail a meeting just as quickly as too many people not talking. If they bring up too many externals, you can still keep things on track by paraphrasing their comments using the framing for the meeting. You either connect their comments back to the main topic or validate their comments and classify them as topics for another meeting. You can interrupt an external. Wait until the person starts to repeat or takes a longer pause. At some point you have to invite others to contribute to keep the rest of the group engaged.

Your company may have meetings in which too many people are silent and others in which too many people say too much. In any group where the conversation is unbalanced, take some time to meet with people offline and run a simple exercise. Ask them, "Do you think out loud? Or do you think before you speak?" Analyze each person's tendency in these situations:

- Under stress
- With your best friends
- With this group

We all vary, but particularly when under stress, people tend toward one kind of thinking or another. When you understand your people's tendencies, you can invite them into conversations when they are silent, and respectfully move the conversation to others' ideas when someone is talking too much.

How to Change Culture Through Meetings: Brian Zanghi and Jennifer Peterson

Founded in 1994, Pragmatech Software shipped its first release in 1995. Pragmatech started out as a desktop application for the individual manager whose job was to build winning proposals to support a large sales organization. In 2005, Pragmatech became a start-up again, completely transforming every aspect of its business, renaming the company Kadient in 2007.

As the CEO at the time, Brian Zanghi described it, "Our new product, Incite Knowledge, was for a sales rep selling products and solutions to other businesses. It put the information that salespeople need to differentiate their products, everything from product information, presentations, proposals, and competitive information to coaching tips and proven selling strategies, online anytime, anywhere. It was a different approach for a different customer."

The transformation of the company into sales enablement as a service started out as a project in R&D and ended up transforming the culture. Zanghi said:

> We set out to build a new product with capabilities to support the needs of a salesperson. We knew that other aspects of the company would be affected down the road, but we stayed in our comfort zone of product development for several months. That changed in 2006—more than a year into the change process. The wake-up call was driven by the completion of the first version of the new product and a recognition that we needed to introduce the product to the market. All aspects of the company were affected.
>
> We were faced with two big challenges in our culture. The first was our need to reduce the size of our workforce to prepare for the financial transition common to companies that change from selling software licenses, where most of the revenue comes up front, to a subscription pricing model. To support this transition, the company had to reduce its spending, and in software, 70 percent of the spending is on the workforce.
>
> The second big challenge was to make sure that we had the right team in the company. Since this business model was relatively new in the industry, the issue wasn't experience as much as it was attitude and persona. We needed a team of people who were comfortable not being comfortable. So much of the work that needed to be done didn't come with a blueprint. It was a trial-and-error process, with lots of experimentation and some mistakes. It takes a certain type of person to thrive in this situation.

Zanghi noted that the culture had to evolve, and quickly:

> When I joined the company in 2004, it had been a bootstrapped operation between 1995 and 2003. Decisions were made from the top down and not explained that well. Because there was no outside financing to serve as a cushion between the ups and down of good quarters and disappointing quarters, the company was managed by the founders and executives quarter to quarter. The environment was schizophrenic. I'd walk into meetings and in response to the uncertainty, people would be

waiting with a piece of paper and a pen—expecting to be told what to do. People were loyal, but they wanted to be told how to fix things.

The new way of communicating began at a meeting on April 1, 2008. Kadient's then head of people strategy, Jennifer Peterson, noticed the moment:

> What became apparent was that there was a gap between the exec team and the leadership team (directors and managers). The exec team had more business experience to tap into, and most of the executives were comfortable in a more active dialogue, but most of the leadership team would freeze when challenged. We had to draw out their internal processing.
>
> The first topic of discussion was first-quarter results. Brian said we fell short of the financial results, but we should feel good about what we did. Initially, no one responded. When directors were specifically asked to respond, their questions and comments were mostly critical. The meeting shut down from there. The execs thought the directors didn't understand or appreciate the progress we had made even though we didn't hit the numbers. The directors thought the execs weren't open to questioning, and everyone left frustrated.

Peterson said that she facilitated two transitions: how and when the company met:

> We quickly did a diagnosis on both sides. We brought the stories together and paid attention to the communication tendencies that were broken. As the group of emerging leaders came together and did the analysis of what our struggles were, we created a set of guidelines of what we needed to be mindful of as we communicated in meetings across the business.
>
> There were things that had gotten us stuck in the past. Naming the issue: we'd talk around the symptoms, and not name the real issue or challenge each other if we disagreed, and we lost a lot of time spinning our wheels. Getting the right people to the table: we had multiple meetings on the same topic because we didn't have the right people to get the

input we needed to make a decision that would stick. Framing conversations: in some of these group meetings, people were trying to figure out where the conversation was going, and then an executive would take control and move it in a different direction because the focus was never framed and what we were trying to accomplish was unclear.

We put these and a few other mantras on a little plastic card and called it our playbook. One day our director of engineering walked into the Thursday meeting and said, "This is my plastic Jesus. I keep it in front of my computer as my reminder." We saw a dramatic impact in four months. Given the change in our staffing model and a team of more emerging, rather than experienced, leaders, the success is how quickly we've been able to transition to this new business while learning to run a whole new organization. As a result of applying these practices, we were able to develop and launch our next product in six months with the company ready to sell, implement, and support it.

The company had added a weekly Thursday meeting for the exec team and the directors, as well as an all-company meeting every Friday. Zanghi revealed the difference between the hierarchical and flat cultures as a result of creating the mantras:

Everyone wore the same hat. As we encouraged open communication where any question was fair game, people spoke and participated without feeling that they will be threatened or punished. It took a while to rid ourselves of the old culture and get to the new place. But to look at how effective an organization can be in dealing with really tough problems when there's a lot of collaboration and trust around the table, it's an amazing thing to watch.

Between 2007 and 2008, Kadient grew its new business by 70 percent, and in the midst of the 2008 economic turmoil, it successfully landed its next round of funding. The company merged in 2010 and was purchased in 2017 for $50 million. The transformations and ultimate successes could not have happened without a culture changed by how they met. Zanghi and Peterson continue their careers as CEO and Chief People Officer of global companies.

How Great Leaders Facilitate Meetings

There's a Bully in the Room

A great facilitator ensures participation. In many meetings, it's common to find someone who is loud and is perceived as a bully. Or maybe this person is internal, but when he makes a comment, even if it's right, it gets personal. He may be doing this on purpose, or he may just be having a bad day. As a facilitator, the way you validate the teammates who struggle establishes your ability to support everyone.

The bully tends to shut down the internal people. The facilitator should first validate what's being said, and then redirect the conversation to create a safe forum for the internal thinkers to speak. For instance, suppose you're the facilitator, and one of the bullies keeps chiming in. You walk a little closer to him as you validate, making eye contact. As you redirect, you move away and change your eye contact to the rest of the room. This is the same thing you do with a heckler in a seminar or presentation—you validate by walking toward him with eye contact. That simple move gives the person disrupting the meeting your attention for a moment. It also shows that you are in control of the room, assuring people that this bully is not going to take over the meeting.

The Boss Cuts You Off

If you have a relationship with your boss where you can tell him directly, "You cut me off in the meeting today. I had an idea that would have made us millions," great. But when you don't have that kind of relationship, you can't just tell him. Some bosses will take offense, and some will get frustrated because they feel you are being insecure. They won't always see their behavior as being a problem for you.

Master communicators first unhook their attitude. If you're still frustrated when you have this conversation, your tone of voice will undermine what you do next. Then, when the meeting is over, you have to speak with your boss in private and say, "How would you like me to communicate if I disagree with you in a meeting?" It's not a question that you ask in public. The question itself, however, is professional. It will strengthen your relationship and the ethos you have in the eyes of the person with more power.

Someone Shuts Down

He could have just lost interest. There may be no deep psychology behind it. It could be that he got a text. It could be that he is intimidated. In the virtual world, their child could need something just beyond the screen. If it's an ongoing thing, you want to talk with that person offline. If you're not his manager, you do what you'd do in the meeting, but do it privately. Say, "I just wanted to follow up and see if you had any other thoughts on today's topic." If you're his manager, you can say, "I noticed that you were pretty quiet in the meeting. Is everything okay?" You're providing a forum for him to build a better relationship with you.

As a facilitator, the way you address everyone else in the meeting will dictate the ability of the person who shut down to participate again. If you validate well, it will create a more comfortable environment for participation, and that person is more likely to participate. There is no magic phrase that will help him. He may be afraid of speaking in public. Remember, a meeting is a kind of public speaking.

Know, however, that the way you respond to another person's totally crazy idea will still decide if that person participates again. If you say, "Well, that's not a good idea," someone who is already a bit uncomfortable speaking in front of the group is far less likely to participate. If you say, "We're getting creative today. What other ideas will solve our problem?" four hands will pop up. One of them will eventually be the person who shut down.

Someone Always Comes to Your Office After the Meeting

Jenny shows up at your door with the idea that would have changed the entire meeting. She has the answer. In her head, she knows exactly what the group needs to focus on. Here she is, 15 minutes after the whole group was together. The group won't be together again until next week. Again, your first move is to validate. She may be internalizing, and you can't fix that by yelling at her or telling her that she should have contributed during the meeting. This is the moment when you can change her behavior by showing her how good she can be.

After validating her idea, ask your first question: "So when did this idea hit you?" If it happened after the meeting, you move on and create a plan for sharing the content. But if she was internalizing during the meeting, say, "Great. What do you need to feel comfortable offering your input when the team's all together?" Comfort is the key. Louder members of the group may have shut her down. She may have a confidence problem. She may be afraid to be wrong and not want to feel embarrassed in front of her peers.

The key to her communicating like a leader is your individual coaching. Follow up before the next meeting to make sure that she knows the topics and understands the issues. Give her brief presentations that are in her sweet spot so that she gains ethos with the group and learns to feel calm when thinking out loud. Ask everyone in the group to give an opinion on a topic so that she isn't singled out. Everyone can learn to externalize, and with your support, her impact on the meetings can change.

If, however, after trying to push her, you don't see the desired results, stop. If she suffers from a fear of speaking, your pushing her to speak up in front of a group will make her more nervous. If you suspect that she is experiencing that level of nervousness, first, know that it's normal. Second, help her get resources like a communication coach or class to develop her level of comfort.

How Do You Know the Format Worked?

People come back. Those who run productive meetings have no problem getting their teammates to show up. The other evidence is that everyone walks out knowing what he owns. Ownership consists of three things: the need, the path, and the deadline.

You meet to fill a need. The purpose statement in the format is a frame of what you're trying to accomplish. If people don't know it, if they can't all tell you the queen of hearts of the meeting, then whatever you talked about is not going to have an impact on how they work.

Once they understand the need, they have to know their part of the path to the solution. They have to do certain things, and they need to be able to say them to you, out loud, after any meeting. Role is not about position in the company. Role is the specific activities a person owns. Few people can be responsible if they can't explain what's expected.

You know that you have deadlines, but did you make them explicit? You need qualified leads for your sales team, for instance. Everyone knows the specific initiatives that they will complete, but do they all understand the urgency? Some projects take years, and others need to be done by 5 p.m. today.

When your team leaves a meeting with clear answers to the simple mantra—*need*, *path*, *deadline*, you know the format worked.

CHAPTER 9

DELEGATION

Delegation is how managers get work done. You can't do it all yourself. A team of one does not scale. When leaders and managers don't delegate clearly, people either sign up for projects that they don't have the ability or the time to do or they simply don't complete the job. In this chapter, you will learn a format that ensures the outcomes you need.

The Third Moment: Delegation

Managers can't do their jobs without delegation. If you manage, at some point you've said, "I tell them what to do, and it never gets done by the deadline." There's something broken in your communication with your team members. Either you weren't clear, or they didn't trust you enough to be honest. They couldn't or wouldn't tell you that they didn't have the time, the resources, or the skills to complete what you needed them to do. Clear delegation sets explicit expectations so that both parties trust that the work will get done. Clear delegation motivates so great work is possible.

The Trap

You don't think things through. You say, "Make 50 cold calls today." Then you expect people to do it. You assume that they have enough clarification and capability to do the task. After all, why would they be in that position if they could not do the work? As a leader or manager of people and projects, however, you need to realize that there may be other factors that either prevent the task from getting done or lead it to be done incorrectly.

Master communicators don't just delegate off the top of their heads. They think through what they need completed and the most effective way to delegate it. Whom are you delegating to? How is that person motivated? What is the best way to communicate the delegation?

When you are in the military, delegation is simple. Subordinates complete tasks because they have been told to do so. If the tasks are not done, the consequences are clear and harsh. In most organizations, you can't take this approach because that's not your culture. You need your teammates to emotionally commit to what you need from them, and the format makes completing projects on time possible.

The Format

1. *Frame the objective.* Fifty cold calls is a task. Three new clients is an objective. What is the result you want the person to produce? When an individual understands the overall objective, he will have an easier time processing the delegation. He will have a context in which he can understand what needs to be done and whether he is capable of meeting the need. It will help him assess whether he has the time to complete the task or not. If you do not communicate what the objective of the delegation is, the person being delegated to may misinterpret the need or its priority.

2. *Match tasks and capabilities.* If Kim is afraid of talking to people, she shouldn't be the person hosting your booth at the trade show. Just because she creates the best displays you've

ever seen and the demo she built is flawless, that doesn't mean that she can give the demo or build relationships with clients. Be honest about what people can do, or they will always disappoint you. This doesn't mean that you don't bring Kim to the trade show and ask her to do one demo for a customer she already knows. Give people objectives where they can be successful, and if you want them to stretch, provide them the resources to train and get better.

3. *Be explicit about limitations.* Think through the limitations in advance, especially those that could be misunderstood. Write them out if you need to. If you have a budget constraint, make that clear during your delegation. Make clear what the person can and cannot do. For example, can he use other employees to help him complete the task? There are times you want your teammate to determine his limitations. As your relationship grows stronger, you will gain more trust in his ability to make those decisions.

4. *Access bandwidth.* You have to determine what you put on each person's plate and what you will take off. More companies than ever before are running at maximum efficiency, even beyond what's possible. Employee engagement continues to challenge most organizations. Some of your employees will always say yes, and now they're overloaded. Some employees spend so much time on one project that others feel like they're not contributing. If you pay attention to bandwidth, people will speak openly with you about their workload. In an ideal world, you want to know if they have so many other things to do that they won't be able to complete the task. If you don't know the scope and time commitment of someone's present workload, ask. After listening, you can prioritize together.

5. *State the deadline.* You'd think this is obvious, but did you say it? Did he say it back to you? Did someone send a follow-up email to make sure that everyone had the same deadline? Does everyone know that it is completely unacceptable to miss a deadline without negotiating the personal reasons why, or getting the team together to explore why more time is

needed? *We are human beings.* Give us two weeks to make a paper airplane, and we will deliver it a minute after the deadline—either because we procrastinated or because we had to make the *perfect* airplane. By the way, we spent 80 hours a week on the airplane project, so you'd better like it. Deadlines are as important as the objective itself. *Tip*: Once the deadline is set, ask, "Is there anything you can think of that would prevent you from meeting this deadline?"

6. **Support them.** If people need help, give it to them. If they need resources, find them. If they need training or coaching, find the funding and time for them. If you've ever heard that great managers develop their people, this is one of those areas when you have a chance to do just that. You won't be able to help unless you know what's happening in their world. *Learn the art of MBWA (management by walking around).* Checking in doesn't mean that you're micromanaging. Walk around the office and ask for brief updates on what people are doing. Start the conversation by saying, "I've got two minutes. Update me on your progress." They have to practice giving quick summaries, and you get to ask a few questions that can support their work. Set the boundary for the conversation (two minutes), ask questions (don't tell them what to do), and do this every day you can.

The Ingredients for a Perfectly Framed Objective

Delegating well is not as simple as saying, "Go do this task." Framing the objective will help you be more focused in your communication and provides the person with a context. Ask yourself four questions:

1. What is the larger objective of what needs to get done?
2. How does this fit into the organization's strategy?
3. What are we trying to accomplish?
4. What resources will the person need?

The answers to these questions don't have to be complicated. You need the answers so the other person truly understands what you need from him.

For instance, you've got a new employee doing payroll. You're in a small company. While you're the vice president of people, you have only two part-time teammates helping you do everything from recruiting and benefits to managing the performance of 50 employees. Imagine that you've just changed to a new payroll processor. You can't just say, "Take care of payroll."

The new person is going to have trouble along the way, so:

1. He needs you to clarify that payroll needs to be done on time so that the other employees know that we value what they do.
2. Even payroll fits into your company's strategy. Imagine that you are trying to introduce your product into a new, specific market. Your salespeople will be getting much bigger reimbursement checks and smaller commissions than normal. You need to explain why. You want everyone on your team to understand how he fits into making the whole organization succeed.
3. He needs to know what he is making happen. In this case, say, "We want to make sure that you learn how to use the new system, that all our numbers match, and that the reports are approved by me and by the CFO before we authorize the payments."
4. Now he knows what to do, and you provide resources. Say, "There is a rep available to help you with the system at this number. You can call the CFO at his office between 12 and 5 o'clock with questions." With the objective clear, you can now set out limitations and the deadline, and be ready to support him further if he needs you.

Each of these objectives has to be stated out loud, followed up by an email and then reclarified in follow-up meetings. Effective delegation can feel like overcommunicating. What feels like overcommunicating is actually just being clear. Being clear up front will save immense amounts of time later when a recurring task or project goes wrong.

The Annual Report

You're the CEO, and you want to delegate the preparation of the annual report to the new CFO. If you're unprepared, you'll say, "You write it, and let's meet next week." You assume that he knows how to prepare an annual report. He's a pro. But you can't assume that your thinking about what goes into the final product matches his expectations. If he's coming from a different company, he may be working from a different model.

Which approach do you think would work better in this case study?

1. *Authoritative.* You can say, "I want these sections to be included." There are cases in which being directive is important. If your relationship is strong enough, this style will probably work well. If you are a hierarchical leader, authoritative communication won't surprise your teammate.
2. *Collegial.* Say, "What sections do you think should go in?" He mentions four: an executive summary, financial statements, an ops update, and a market segment review. You want the report to have additional sections. So you ask, "What have the best annual reports looked like in your past companies?" Through the discussion you end up agreeing to add the R&D plan and new product plans.

In most delegations, at every level, collegiality about the objective creates the most connection. The approach you take in each delegation, however, depends on the listener. Some people want to be part of defining the objective, and others just want to know what needs to get done. Sometimes you need to be authoritative to avoid confusion. In this example, the collegial approach is best because you want to get to know and build trust with your new colleague.

Completing the format, you don't ask your CFO whether he's capable of preparing an annual report. If your CFO can't do it, you have a bigger problem. You do still need to be definitive about limitations, in this case the number of pages. Think you don't have to make page count clear at the C-suite level? If you don't, you could get the shortest or the longest report ever. The details that matter to you as the delegator are the details you need to make distinct in the delegation.

Then you ask a simple question that covers the fourth and fifth steps of the format: "In your schedule, do you have time to get this done by Friday?" If the CFO trusts you, he will tell you honestly. But he is new. If he does not tell you, watch his body language. If he has too much to do, he will tense up. Another assessment statement is, "Tell me about your workload right now."

Exploring his present responsibilities sets the table for a conversation about supporting him. If the CFO has never written the new product review, and you need this section, ask, "How comfortable are you with doing the new product review?" Your skill is to identify what he needs through questions and then offer support. At every level of an organization, people need support.

But remember, if you're giving someone too much help, and the project isn't strategic training so that he won't need your help in the future, that's not delegating. You're doing the work.

How Google Delegates: Laszlo Bock

As vice president of people operations, Laszlo Bock led every aspect of how Googlers work together. To create clear expectations, decision making at Google is a process, as Bock related:

> The actual moment when you make a decision is actually less important than the process by which you get there. At Google, and in my own experience, what works best is engaging in debate and discussion all along the way, so that by the time you're actually giving direction, in 95 percent of the cases, everybody already says, "Of course that's what we're going to do, and of course we're in agreement." And even if you're not in complete agreement, the response is, "I understand why we view this issue differently, and while our direction is not my view, I understand that it's the consensus view and it makes sense and I will execute it faithfully." Often, you don't even give direction; the team decides and delivers.

Too many leaders and managers don't value the many ways in which people can do great work or truly trust their people to produce. Bock knows how to build trust and get the results he expects:

> People often believe that there is one key to success. I believe that there are many paths. In general, I deliberately leave the end product somewhat vaguely defined, and the trade-off I'm making is that while it will almost certainly be somewhat different from what the result would be if I were doing the task directly, the result will be a more full expression of what the people who are working on it believe is the right answer. Not only does that generate a very good, high-quality outcome, but it's often a better outcome than I could have come up with if I had done it on my own.

Bock is intentional about building the trust from the beginning of a relationship that allows him to believe in his people and for them to feel that they can take the risks. "The way you get to that point where you can avoid being overly prescriptive," Bock said, "is to go through a calibration period. My style is always trust first."

But trust doesn't mean that managing isn't important. "If you're shown that the outcome is not what you need, then you manage more tightly," explained Bock. "It's always been a process of 'Let's see what the person does,' and then you coach and guide. There will always be a set of cases where you need to define exactly the results you need."

The Best Paths to Results

When to Delegate Versus When to Do It Yourself

A big question for leaders and managers is, "When do I delegate, and when do I do it myself?" In theory, as a manager, *you always delegate*. When you get busy, one of the problems is that you start diving in and doing the work yourself because you have to. That's fine, but now you're not managing, you're doing. On smaller teams, often the manager is also a doer. The secret to your success is learning how to trust people and then finding or growing people who understand how to receive your messages about what needs to get done.

A lot of times you do the work because you know how to get it done right. This results in your not making the time to coach and train your people so that they are in a place where you can delegate to them. If you're constantly correcting people's work, ask yourself why it is being done incorrectly. Maybe they don't have the skill set. Maybe you haven't communicated all of the components required to ensure that they know exactly what to do. That's the value of the format.

In the purest sense of a manager delegating, the only time you do the work yourself is when you are coaching or teaching your teammate how to do something. If the person has never done it before, do it together, trading drafts back and forth. It's okay to do that once, maybe twice, so that the third time he owns the project. You're doing the work because you are developing a fellow leader.

The only other time is when there is no one else to do it. In a lot of companies when the economy is tight or if you are in a start-up business, you may have a small staff. You won't have the luxury of practicing management in its purest form. You can still strive toward it as you grow and develop your business. If you're in an environment where the culture is to show that you can do the hard work too, you take on part of the load. But for most managers most days the goal is to same: spend your time leading because you delegated effectively.

Should You Get Them Flowers?

Should you say thank you? There has to be a form of validation after you delegate in all cases, but how you say thank you depends on people's motivation. Sometimes it's as simple as a head nod in private. Other times it is a trophy at the company meeting. People need confirmation that they have done the right thing. The problem with gratitude usually isn't saying thank you too much, it is not saying it enough.

But saying thank you can backfire. When the person you're saying thank you to feels so much a part of the team, he may say, "Of course I did this. Why are you thanking me?" In this case, the problem isn't that you validated him. It is how. The person may have just needed a head nod or even the next assignment. If you never said thank you to your peers and you win the promotion, don't start saying thank you. They will say, "Now you have to say thank you." When thank you isn't the right answer, find the ways of appreciation that are creative and work for each person's unique needs.

Micromanaging

Micromanaging is a trust issue: you don't trust your people to get the work done. You don't believe that they can do the job, so you have to set up situations in which they can prove themselves to you. If someone cannot write the annual report well, how long are you going to let that go on before you do something about it? *Either train him, send him to a class, move him to another place in the company, or lose him.* Don't just say, "I told him how to do it," and expect this to be enough. For some people it might be, but if this person's behavior is not changing, consider developing him in another way. Otherwise, you'll be micromanaging. That means that you're doing the work, not managing. Recognize that you're doing it and come up with a strategy to stop.

There's only one way to get out of micromanagement if you work for someone: prove that you can do the work. Use the techniques and the formats to communicate with your boss so that he understands that you are talented and capable. Then, when you tell him that the report will be in on Monday at 9:00, turn it in on Monday at 9:00. If it comes in at 9:05, no excuse in the world will matter. It's just late. If he doesn't say anything, that's even worse because he is thinking it.

You, the one who wants to prove to your boss that he can trust you, need to be on top of every single communication. After about a month or two, your boss will treat you differently. But it takes concentrated effort to communicate your information to him exactly the way *he* wants it. In most cases when you're being micromanaged, more information is better. *Be on time, be on task, and be in communication.* If your boss doesn't treat you differently over time, and this bothers you, look to leave your position or switch managers because it is no longer a trust issue. Your boss has an ego issue, and your boss will probably never change.

Suppose you are a manager or leader who says, "*No!* My career is on the line. I have to get involved when it's not being done right." Getting in the weeds sometimes is not micromanagement. We know that there are situations where you need to get involved. Micromanaging is telling someone what to do every step of the way. Too much of it turns your employees off, burns you out, and is simply inefficient management.

Delegating to an Equal

Earn the permission to delegate. You don't pull rank on your equal unless it's been predetermined that you're leading a project. You never want to sound like you're telling an equal what he has to do. When a relationship is strong enough, a business partner will say, "Okay, you're the boss. Tell me what to do." Those are rare moments and rarer people.

If you're at a meeting, and Steven is put in charge of a group of equals, what happens next depends on Steven's ethos. If Steven is the natural leader, no problem. But if Steven is not the natural leader, he has to develop the relationship with the others first. He has to frame the relationship with each person who gives him permission to delegate. He has to say, "Okay, Bill, how do you want to move forward? We haven't worked like this together, and I'm responsible for the project. What's the best way for me to delegate?" You have to reach out before you have work to delegate and ask the others in the group, "What's the best way for us to work together?"

Then, go back and use the format—but not until you have permission.

Delegating to Someone Who Doesn't Report to You

Take the person to lunch or grab a coffee first. If you haven't built a relationship with someone so that you know her communication tendencies, your ethos with her, and what motivates her, delegation becomes a demand. Master communicators begin with exploration. Asking for someone's help without knowing how she thinks and what's important to her is delegating in the dark.

You may need to meet with someone's manager first. Ask the question, "When we need something from each other's teammates, how do you want me to be in touch with you to make sure they have the bandwidth?"

When delegating to someone on another team, ask, "What work are you curious about in addition to your daily commitments?" or "What work do you love doing?" And don't be afraid to ask, "Do you have bandwidth these days?" You can't give work to someone on another team if she doesn't have time to do it. You're just dumping work on the other teams unless you know what the other people care about and the work that's important to them.

How Do You Know the Format Worked?

The work is completed properly, on time, and the results may even be better than you expected. When you delegate effectively, you notice people anticipate the work that needs to be done. Delegations become easier and require less explanation. Your teammates will innovate because they no longer need to figure out what you want them to do. Instead they put their best thinking into improvement. When you notice a strained relationship or a teammate who consistently misses deadlines or details, adjust how you communicate the tasks. Revisit the individual's ability to complete the work. Delegation clarity creates results.

CHAPTER 10

FEEDBACK

Feedback is communicating about the need to change or sustain behaviors. When it's done badly, leaders and managers demotivate their teammates. Not only does the behavior not change, but the relationship gets worse. In this chapter, you will learn the format for providing feedback in a direct way and what to say when a teammate's performance doesn't improve.

The Fourth Moment: Feedback

With trust, providing feedback can be comfortable and often produces the results you need. But what about when you're dealing with a new employee? What about someone you've struggled with or another manager's team member? When you see problems with the behavior of a member of your team, when is the right moment to speak up? Too much feedback, and you're a micromanager. Not enough, and your people can lose their focus wondering how they are doing.

Your team is the group of people that makes you successful. As the leader, you can see when things are going in the right direction toward the vision. Where you give the feedback matters too. One comment in a meeting in front of everyone can prevent someone from telling you what he really thinks for months, if not forever. As you see your people thrive, you need to provide feedback to reinforce them. When they struggle, you need to provide feedback to correct their behavior. Your team members are trying to fulfill the vision or complete tasks. If you can't give meaningful feedback, they can't do their best work.

The Trap

You don't want to make your people uncomfortable. You think they can't take it. You don't tell them what you really think, and then when you do, it comes out wrong. Or you make the opposite mistake: you think your relationship is strong enough for them to hear your criticism, but your criticism is so direct that they become defensive.

Feedback can be a habit that's as addictive as smoking. When you realize that your teammates will perform better, you will offer it more often. When you know that they won't be angry and, in fact, they are grateful for your opinion, feedback becomes a normal part of your team. When you deliver your opinion of their work effectively, you help them learn. Not every piece of feedback needs to be given, but keeping critical information to yourself hurts their growth.

But remember the power dynamic. If you are the leader or manager with a higher level of authority, check your ethos. Don't give feedback as buddies. You're not their friend; you're their boss. You control their child's college tuition. That doesn't mean that you have to be formal or distant. You have to have a clear pattern you follow consistently so they can hear you invite them to be better on an ordinary day and you can discipline people when they must change.

Did the word *discipline* trigger you? Even if you are a teacher, discipline is not something most of us like to do. That's why the format is so important. When you are comfortable delivering feedback, the behaviors change before the more formal communication moments are necessary.

The Format

1. *Describe the specific behavior.* You don't need to sugarcoat it, but an "I statement" is important. "I experienced you" and "I noticed that you" are examples of stock phrases that identify

what you want to be different. If you say, "You did this" or
"You did that," the person gets defensive. The royal "We
noticed" is condescending. Use an I statement to be direct
and specific, and you have the greatest chance of the person
understanding what went wrong.

2. **Describe the result of the behavior.** You manage a call center.
You've just described the behavior. "Tom, I've noticed that
you're coming in at 9:15 a.m." Notice that you didn't say,
"coming in 15 minutes late." That frame immediately creates
defensiveness. Imagine that he didn't know that when he came
in mattered to you or the team. At your weekly one-on-one,
you bring it up. The next comment needs to be what happens
because of the behavior: "The team is getting behind every
morning, and our response time to customers is suffering."

3. **Describe the desired correct behavior.** Decide if you need
to be didactic or Socratic. The didactic approach is direct.
An I statement is usually enough: "I need you here at 8:55."
"We need you here by 8:55" has more authority because it
speaks for the team. Use *we* only when you have to place extra
emphasis on the correction. The Socratic approach is more
inductive. Ask questions like, "What is getting in the way of
arriving at 9:00?" or "Help me understand what's in the way of
arriving at 9:00?" The goal is to help the other person uncover
the reasons he struggles so he can make the correction.

Which approach is better? It depends on the urgency and
your leadership style. Quick corrections need direct feedback,
and questions are better if you have time. Hierarchical leaders
are often direct, where flatter leaders more often use a Socratic
approach.

These first three points by themselves are feedback. Deliver
them in an unapologetic and direct tone. The person you're
talking to will get the message. If you're delivering feedback
for the first time, stop here and ask him, "So what needs to be
different in our work together?" He needs to be able to repeat
the three points in his own words. If he can't, he didn't hear
you, and you have to do it again.

4. **Describe *your criteria for judgment.*** Feedback escalates to the formal communication called discipline when you add Steps 4 and 5 of the format. If the person continues to come in late, tell him how you will determine that he is improving. "Tom, when you come in each morning at 8:55, swing by my office first to let me know you're here." If the improvement has data attached, let him know the metric you will be tracking. He can't know what to work on if you aren't clear about what you are measuring.

5. *Describe the consequences of repeat behavior.* This is the most difficult step for most managers because it makes most of us uncomfortable. It doesn't have to be. People can't succeed if you don't tell them what will happen if they don't change the way they work. "Tom, if you're not in my office at 8:55 every morning this week, we'll explore helping you find a work environment that better fits your work style."

Consequences need to be understood, believed, and cared about. If people don't get what will happen if they don't change, they can't alter their behavior. If they think you are bluffing, they won't alter their behavior. If they don't care, they can't even begin to appreciate what needs to be different. Consequences have to be clear, real, and matter to make a difference.

This collective approach is so simple and so practical that it seems silly. Now check the last time you wanted someone to work differently. Did you tell him? If you did, how did you tell him? Did his performance change? When you use this format repeatedly, if his performance doesn't change, you know that he may not be right for your team.

I Shouldn't Have to Tell Him

If you're a leader or a manager, you don't want to have to tell your people what they are doing wrong. You're not their parent. They should just know. They should take ownership of the work that needs to get done and be as excited to excel as you are. They may be and simply may not understand your expectations. Or they may not be, and you need to figure out what's causing their poor performance. Either way, they can't read your mind.

Ironically it is by honestly and constructively telling people what they do wrong and how to improve that relationships get better over time. It starts with simple conversations about your most basic expectations. When Tom from the previous section keeps coming in late, he's probably not doing it on purpose. And even if it's happening because he is careless, does he truly understand that he always needs to arrive at 8:55? The way you have this conversation builds the trust you need so that when you ask for something in the future, it happens without constant follow-up.

For instance, instead of a call center, suppose you manage a bank. In giving Tom feedback, you say, "I need to talk to you about when you come into the office. When you do that, people look at you like you're getting special treatment. I'd like you to get here a few minutes early so that we can change that perception." Notice the framing.

> **Step 1.** *Describe the specific behavior.* Again, telling him that he's late creates defensiveness, whereas talking about when he comes into the office gives you a chance to get into the behavior.
>
> **Step 2.** *Describe the result of the behavior.* Your focusing on the perception caused by what he is doing allows him to see that. While he didn't realize it, his present hours prevent him from building effective relationships with the other members of the team.
>
> **Step 3.** *Describe the desired correct behavior.* Getting here a few minutes early so that he can change the perception isn't threatening. It's direct and clear about what you need and what will happen to his ethos with his coworkers when he works differently.

Most managers struggle to deliver this kind of direct message, but let's say that you give feedback this clearly as soon as the right arena presents itself. Let's also say that this is the third time you've had the exact same conversation. You say, "I love the work you're doing on [name a specific project], and I don't want this to get in the way. I want you to call me at 8:30 for the next two weeks to make sure everything is going smoothly. I'm not doing this because I want to be a jerk, but if your arrival time doesn't change, this will affect your performance review and your year-end bonus."

> ***Step 4.*** *Describe your criteria for judgment.* Notice the validation before asking for a phone call. Make your teammate do the work, but let him know what you're looking for. You didn't say for a *few* weeks, you said for *two* weeks because when you are disciplining someone, you have to be specific.

> ***Step 5.*** *Describe the consequences of repeat behavior.* Saying that it will affect his performance review is the truth. Tell him. If you don't tell him what is going to happen, he can't change. We're repeating this advice because it is so rarely followed. No member of your team should ever be surprised by your expectations. If someone is, you never told him exactly what will happen if he doesn't perform.

Your best employees will respond immediately to criticism given in this format, but two-thirds of your team aren't your best. They need the format even more so that they get used to how you deliver information on what they need to improve. This produces one of two exceptionally important results: they perform better, or, if they can't, don't, or won't, they won't be surprised when you invite them to explore a new work environment where they can succeed.

This doesn't just come to you. When you're going to have a feedback conversation, go into your office and decide, "How am I going to follow the five steps?" Test out the conversation with a colleague or a trusted advisor to see if you are using any loaded words that will distract from your message. Is this just feedback, or is it more serious and it's time to help the person discipline his behavior?

Sometimes, after writing out what you want to say and practicing it, you realize that this is not a moment for feedback. Maybe defensive persuasion or another technique would be better. We hear the word *discipline* and think of children getting punished; this is about performance improvement. You're not punishing someone when you tell him what you'll measure and what consequences will follow continued failures. You give the person an insanely clear chance to succeed.

As you decide your frames, write them out. You can't just do this off the cuff, even if you know the format by heart. Write the frames as if you're preparing the frames of a meeting. Then practice your delivery into your smartphone. Listen for your tone. Does it match your meaning? Do you sound the way your father did when he criticized you? Laugh at yourself, and then find the respectful voice that will connect to your employee. Your preparation is a sign of your strength and your desire to be a master communicator.

How to Give Effective Direct Feedback: Mark Russell

Mark Russell is a turnaround expert. "When I come in," he told us, "the existing executive management team either is not well formulated or lacks clear accountability. In either case, to execute a successful turnaround effort, you need a clear vision and a hill to climb together. I always stress that my job is to *help* fix things. It is my team's job to fix them."

If having a hill to climb together is part of Russell's mission, communication at Wunderman Team Detroit, where Russell was president for five years, was a mountain. He managed 350 team members providing all of the digital and direct marketing for Ford Motor Corporation and several divisions within it. Adding to the complexity, Wunderman was one of the five marketing agencies owned by parent company WPP working collaboratively on Ford's marketing efforts (the others were JWT, Young & Rubicam, Ogilvy & Mather, and MindShare).

The challenge within any agency of this magnitude, where innovation is paramount and creativity is a collaborative project across several teams, is making sure that communication flows to all employees.

Every team must know what the others are doing and share constant feedback. Russell noted that:

> Some team members have exclusionary tendencies and like to take the ball and run with it. Working with over a thousand people and multiple sister agencies, we needed inclusive behavior and collaborative process; doing anything in a vacuum does not work. If you neglect to bring people along with your deliverables, get buy-in, input, and feedback throughout the process, things can and will break down.
>
> When that has happened, I have had to sit down with that individual or team and point out the result, the ripple effects it had throughout the agency, and how much time it took to correct and fix it.

A major challenge for a leader in a turnaround situation or during the course of everyday business is to deliver feedback so that the team or individual understands what needs to be changed. Russell observed:

> It's a fallacy that there are born leaders. Leadership is learned. Leadership is about relationships. A good leader must clearly understand their individual team members and what motivates them. He or she must understand how each person thinks, why they behave a particular way, respect where they come from, and consider their perspective. By doing so the leader will build a relationship of trust, can deliver constructive, motivating feedback, and can coach individuals into the mindset that this is a team sport.
>
> When someone is particularly a challenge, the setup is all-important. You must get this person into a mindset where they understand the context of where you're coming from. Then, knowing that you are dealing with a particular individual, understand that one approach to feedback does not fit all. You must tailor the delivery and message so that it can be well received. Lastly, "perception is reality." Following feedback, many people will come back with excuses for what happened. If they argue the feedback, I present it in a way where it's not really an option. I say whether or not you think you're justified, it doesn't matter: Here is the criticism; these are the perceptions of what people are telling me. This is how you were perceived. Perception is reality.

Russell knows the risk of not giving effective feedback:

I think the leadership roles I play are "elected positions." I'm voted in, and if my constituency is not happy with my decisions, then I may get voted out, as I should. At the end of the day, it is about the health of the agency.

Ultimately, my management team becomes a reflection of my core beliefs and process. This change takes time and consistent reinforcement. I provide a clear message and a context about why I require people to approach things as I do. By doing so, I mold a group of highly motivated individuals into a cohesive team, and together we climb our next hill.

Feedback Builds Trust

What Tone Should I Use?

In the military or in a life-or-death situation like an emergency room, you use a commanding tone. You give clear, aggressive direction as the situation demands. In most work environments, however, if you yell at people, or if you speak to them like an unhappy adult from their childhood, they will stop trusting you.

You want to match your tone to the situation. If you're too demanding in your tone, it can weaken their trust. When you ask someone questions in a genuinely curious tone to explore what you want him to do differently, he will be less defensive. Instead of feeling that you have to reprimand the person, you get to figure out what will improve the situation next time.

Give the person a chance to discuss what went wrong in his own words. Create a dialogue on why this is happening, and what he can do about it himself. As you engage in that dialogue, let the format's structure guide you. Take your time. The format will ensure that feedback is effectively delivered. Your willingness to discuss what happened will lower his defensiveness and increase the chance of behavioral change.

Performance Reviews

Performance reviews are the perfect example of what goes wrong in organizations. When reviews are done well, they improve engagement. Done poorly, they damage relationships. There are best practices for reviews no matter what your company's platform or style.

The golden rule with a performance review is "no surprises." Your teammate comes in with anxiety, hoping for a good score and perhaps a bonus. If you have a judgmental opinion of his performance over the past month, six months, or year, it can't come out for the first time in a review. Not only will the person either shut down or get angry, he will tell the world what a terrible leader you are.

This is easily avoided. Stay in touch with your teammates throughout each quarter. Make the time to take them to lunch or have informal feedback sessions. Some managers hold weekly check-ins just to stay connected. You can use the formal performance review as a tool to make sure your feedback is clear. You can say something like, "Your formal performance review is in two months. If I had to score you today, it would be a 3. I'd love to see you at a 5, and here is what I need to see you do." With this approach, your teammate knows what your goals for him are, and he can do something about it. Plan regular feedback so that the performance review is "just another meeting."

With no surprises and appropriate anxiety, this is still a conversation about money and the future. Make the review a chance to explore where your colleague wants to go professionally. If you make the review about the future and regular check-ins about improvement and generating good ideas, you will see your relationships strengthen and performance rise. We've seen this not only in the United States but also around the world. The corporate culture that makes performance improvement a regular topic of conversation allows feedback, done well, to become a driver of better results.

Should You Criticize Your Boss?

The president of an international multibillion-dollar Asian company in the camera and film industry enjoys public speaking. He engaged a communication advisor to strengthen and develop his style. As he finished up his practice speech, he reached the part where he thanked certain individuals. When he said, "Thank you," because he was speaking English with a thick Asian accent, the word *thank* sounded like a well-known four-letter expletive. His advisor almost fell out of her seat. Of course, she stopped him immediately, and shared with him what word he appeared to be producing. He did not understand what he was doing wrong, so she wrote down the word on a piece of paper.

He did not say a word. He sat back in his chair and stared at her in anger for about three minutes. He was not angry with her. In fact, she became a friend for life. He was angry with his direct reports. They knew that his accent was creating an embarrassing moment, maybe even damaging his ethos. They had not told him. His staff members were so afraid of him that they could not provide the feedback he needed. He pondered this as he reflected on the various strange looks he had received in the past. He frowned as he processed how many times he had insulted people.

Giving Feedback to Your Boss

The same format works when you give feedback to your boss or someone in a higher position in your organization. Where you do it, however, is paramount. Talk to him in private first. This is different from disagreeing. If you disagree with your boss, and your culture wants people to speak up immediately, frame your challenge and let the debate begin.

Feedback is different. In an ideal world, senior management wants regular direct, deductive feedback. If you're not in that situation, you need to be more strategic. For instance, suppose you're a vice president of operations. The problem is that your CEO has not been present, and it's affecting morale. You're in a 150-person business that has doubled in size in the last year. You're in a fund-raising cycle, so the CEO has been meeting with potential investors all over the world. But you keep hearing comments from people wondering where he's been. The reality is simple: he used to manage by walking around. With so many new employees, he can't have as much face time with everyone. That doesn't change the perception. He's losing ethos, and you can help.

Use the first three steps of the feedback format and have a personal conversation. Open with a validation about the fund-raising. Ask him to tell you what he's been doing. This immediately proves that you know how hard he has been working. Bosses need that from their teams as much as every other teammate does. Then name the behavior: "Folks have noticed that you're not around as much." Cite the result: "I'm hearing people wonder if something's wrong." The final step is the key. Talk about how you hope to work together to change the perception. "I wanted to explore how we can maximize the impact of your face time so that people get the benefit of your leadership." When you approach your boss as a partner wanting to explore how to make him more effective, your ethos goes up, and you improve the culture where you work.

Should I Ever Single Someone Out in a Meeting?

Yes, if the person is being disruptive in a public way and needs to stop. Yes, in a small, highly competitive environment where the employees are so committed that the public humiliation will drive them to do better. Calling someone out in a meeting can also work if your employee is an ethos- and power-motivated person, who will see aggressive public feedback as a sign of respect that pushes him to perform better.

But this is a specific personality type. If you don't already understand this kind of person, if what we're saying doesn't make sense to you, don't single someone out. A military drill instructor uses angry, penetrating tones to embarrass someone so that he doesn't make the same mistake again. In almost every other environment, this tactic will backfire. Managers get confused. You think being a tough manager means holding people accountable. So you play tough with a member of your team at a meeting. Feedback only works if it is heard. A culture of feedback is only effective when the direct criticism has appropriate tone and the team believes you want them all to improve. When you call someone out, and they aren't ready, *your* ethos goes down.

How Do You Know the Format Worked?

People's behavior changes. They can repeat what you told them and why it matters in their own words. At the end of any feedback session, you want to ask, "What are the most important points from our conversation?" If the first three steps of the format worked, the person will be able to tell you what needs to be different, what problem his behavior was causing, and how he is going to work more effectively. If it's a discipline situation, he will also be able to tell you how you are going to measure the change and what's on the line if he can't or won't improve. If people can't repeat back the steps of the format, continue the conversation until they can. Mutual clarity is the first key to behavior change.

CHAPTER 11

PRESENTATIONS

Almost every time you open your mouth and share your ideas, you are making a presentation. Poor presentations disengage listeners and send the wrong message. In this chapter, you will learn the best practices used by thousands of organizations around the world to organize, plan, and deliver spoken content.

The Fifth Moment: Presentations

We have to get personal for a moment. It's possible to give a compelling presentation even if you don't like doing it. As people who spend our lives public speaking and helping other people speak better, we need you to hear something and believe us. You can do this. We've helped people go from boring to engaging and from nervous to enthusiastic. It's not necessary for every word to be smooth. The best presentations don't always go off without a hitch. You may not think that you can improve, but you can. In order to manage and lead people effectively, you have to.

The Trap

You don't prepare. It's that simple. The format for giving presentations reveals the essential places where you have to focus on what you say and how you say it. Give too much information, and your audience may become overwhelmed. If you present badly, they will stop paying attention. Fail to emphasize the most important words and ideas properly, and your audience won't retain your point. Practice the wrong way, and you won't feel comfortable with your content. Your body language and tone will suggest that you aren't ready. Your audience will feel the material isn't important. If you're giving a team presentation and you don't prepare together, you will be a bunch of people with the same business card, but not a team.

The Format

1. *Identify the type of presentation you are giving.* It's not one size fits all. A budget review is very different from an inspirational talk. This isn't brain surgery; it's being clear about what you have to prepare. See "The Different Kinds of Presentations" later in this chapter where we've put together an exhaustive list of the most common types of presentations and the clear ways you can prepare for them.

2. *Decide on a theme.* What's the one thing you want your listeners to remember—your main point? This is your takeaway—that clear, declarative sentence framing what you're saying. *You need to be able to state it in less than 10 words.* This is the chorus you come back to over and over.

   Use the theme as your test. In theory, you ought to be able to reconnect to your theme after every example or subject change. If you can't understand how a story or a point ties to the theme, neither will your listeners. That means either that the theme is off or that this particular information, while exciting and important, doesn't fit into this presentation. In general, you should say the theme at least three times: at the beginning, middle, and end of the presentation. Whether you say it more than that depends on your speaking style. There are some presentations where you can have more than one theme, but you should never have more than three. Your listeners simply won't retain more than that, and you risk them losing all your messages because of overload.

3. ***Decide on illustrations.*** Everything that supports your theme has to be there on purpose. As you explore your content, think about how each story, piece of data, example, or editorial will contribute to your main theme.

4. ***Write it out.*** You can write your presentation word for word or just sketch an outline or mind map. Use what works for you. The act of writing it down will formalize your thoughts and help expose areas that need to be adjusted. Even if you're not going to use the notes when you actually present, this is where you force yourself to make choices. You can use your computer or the back of an envelope and scraps of paper, as some say Lincoln did when writing the Gettysburg Address. There is no one size that fits all, but to be effective, you have to prepare.

5. ***Consider visual aids.*** This is a huge problem in business presentations. If you use visuals such as PowerPoint or Keynote, you need to keep them simple and supportive. The only reason you want to project something 10 feet high or screen share in a virtual meeting is to emphasize something you say. The error too many people make is writing their PowerPoint visuals as bulleted lists of full sentences. Then you project that file, and the visuals become too much information for listeners to digest. More on visual aids in the "Visuals" section.

6. ***Practice your delivery.*** You need to become familiar and comfortable with what you are going to say and, just as important, how you will say it. This does not happen by thinking about it. You have to do it. *You don't need to memorize.* Remember, you're not an actor. It's okay to use notes, and you should mark your notes to cue yourself and adjust your delivery.

In general, we've found that when you *practice six times,* you'll see an improvement. The first rounds are about adjustments. The final work is about synchronizing words with visuals and body language. Don't feel that practicing is slacking off from real work or tell yourself that you don't have the time. Practicing is part of doing your job. Book a conference room. You don't have to practice the whole presentation. If your time is limited, practice your transitions from the four-step outline we're about to teach you. When you're giving an hour-long presentation, it's often not practical to practice the whole thing six times, for a total of six hours. But you can practice the transitions six times in an hour. When you know the order and how you will make the transitions, your familiarity will produce comfort.

The Four-Step Outline

This is what you write out to organize your thoughts. If you use it every time you give a presentation, your audience will always remember your message. Master communicators can do this on the fly. Someone can ask you a question about anything, and you can give an answer that makes sense by following this pattern of thinking.

In *all* cases, your presentation should be well organized. The four-step outline works in all presentations. How you implement it depends on your style. It works for everything from informal presentations, such as a wedding toast, to formal presentations, such as financial reviews, Board meetings, and product updates. The titles of the four steps will become your mantra for remembering what makes any presentation effective.

1. *Tell what tell.* Tell your listeners what you're going to be talking about—the length of your presentation, your topic, and any other special instructions. You have to do this because then they relax. They know what to expect, and they can settle into listening to you.
2. *Tell why they should listen.* This is a brief statement about why these people should be listening to you. It's not necessarily why they should agree with you or why they

should buy what you're selling them, but why should they be paying attention. This is the "what's in it for me" step. Even if they don't like you or like your topic, they will understand why you're talking about it. Even if they already know why they should be listening, this will remind them and get them thinking, "I'm in the right place for the right reason."

In a keynote speech, for example, Step 2 could be a 10-minute story, with that whole story being about why they should listen to you. In most business meetings, it's just a brief statement. The stronger your Step 2, the more engaged your listeners are going to be. Remember, you can speak at around 183 words per minute, but they can process 600. You control what they are thinking about with the 400 words bouncing around in the back of their heads when you give them compelling reasons why what you're saying matters.

3. *Tell.* This is the body of your presentation, where you will spend most of your time. It includes stories, examples, editorials, and emotional appeals to your audience. But remember, people won't hear any of this if they can't relax and understand why to listen (Step 2).

4. *Tell what has been told.* This is your summary. A summary includes two parts: first, you summarize your most important points, and second, you provide an action statement when applicable—what you want your listeners to do now that they know this information. A summary does not contain everything, and you are not repeating yourself. None of us remembers everything we hear the first time. Repetition is essential for retention.

When you use the four-step outline, you outline not only your entire presentation, but each topic you discuss. The entire outline repeats itself again and again throughout the presentation. As a result, even if you are nervous, when you are well organized, your listeners appreciate it and experience you as effective.

Don't wing the four-step outline unless you know what you're doing. A master chef can walk into a kitchen, take various ingredients, and produce a delicious meal on the fly. He can do it because he's spent time learning the various attributes of the different ingredients. He knows what tomatoes will taste like at various temperatures, and how they will mix with greens. Master communicators are just as familiar with the various attributes of human communication. They know that even though they have been presenting for 30 years, practicing will give them more impact. Until you reach that level, don't wing it. Practice it.

Presenting to Those Above You

Your boss has just told you that you will be presenting to the senior management of the company. It's up to you to deliver an update on the project you're working on to secure continued funding and resources. If you nail it, you can hire the resources you need to bring your vision to reality. If you don't, your project may be stopped.

While executives are different all over the world, we've found that these rules produce the strongest ethos in most settings:

1. Prepare your presentation in sections, with each section following the four-step outline.
2. Be prepared to jump around, connecting each section to your main point.
3. Ask listeners if there is a particular topic they would like you to start with or make sure that you cover.
4. Don't take offense if they stop you abruptly. Your comfort with their interruptions reveals your confidence.

You may not have to adapt your presentation. Be comfortable enough with the content and the order of your slides so you can. The stress reaction we all experience when we are surprised is what you want to avoid through preparation. When practicing, have a colleague ask you to jump to the end of your presentation or something in the middle. Have the person interrupt you as you're making an important point. Practicing how to recover from being thrown off makes the disruption an opportunity to show your poise and confidence.

The Different Kinds of Presentations

This is your cheat sheet. Presentations have an impact on the largest number of people at one time. In each section, we will tell you the best approach, what to expect from your audience, and the biggest mistake most people make. The most common types of formal presentations in organizations are:

- *Updates or briefings. Approach:* It should be deductive, well structured, and organized point by point. *Audience:* You might consider starting your presentation by framing the parameters of what you are prepared to talk about and then invite requests for changes to the agenda. Be ready to jump around in your content. *The biggest mistake:* Not being prepared to be interrupted. Be prepared to be interrupted, and welcome interruptions because they show that you know what you're talking about.
- *Sales presentations. Approach:* These presentations are emotion-driven, focus on benefits, and should never describe a feature without following with a benefit. *Audience:* Again, be prepared to be interrupted, and welcome it. Make sure your presentation is about your listeners. Invite them to share what they want you to focus on. *The biggest mistake:* You are not there to train them, and you could risk providing too much information.
- *Conference presentations. Approach:* They should be theme-based. Begin with a story that leads to a theme, supported by a structured outline of your logic. *Audience:* You probably will not be interrupted. Take your time, show everyone how happy you are to get the chance to talk with them (whether it's a smaller or a bigger crowd than you expected), and enjoy matching the emotion in your speech with the emotion in your content. *The biggest mistake:* You go into one topic too deeply. You're providing a generalist's perspective so that they will want to know more later.
- *Keynote presentations. Approach:* These presentations are challenging—more on this in a moment. *Audience:* People are

excited to listen because you're kicking things off. *The biggest mistake:* This is one of the more misunderstood presentations. Many conferences offer multiple keynotes. *Keynote* is a term, a metaphor from the keynote in an orchestra. One individual provides the keynote for other musicians to use to tune their instruments.

In a keynote presentation, it's the same thing. The keynote should set the tone for the rest of the conference. It's not just that the speaker is a big name. The presentation provides a key theme. The best keynote presentations will pose the challenging questions and concepts for the rest of the conference. A keynote speaker should be inspirational and informational. He should have insight and knowledge about the topic of the conference. His "theme" should tie into those of all the other speakers at the event. The listeners often pose questions, but the speaker *shouldn't* answer them. Instead, he should inspire the listeners to seek the answers through the other speakers and events at the conference.

- *Town hall presentations. Approach:* The leader or manager kicking off a town hall meeting must give a presentation. This should be similar to the keynote presentation. Set the tone, excite, and then inspire people to participate. *Audience:* You need to have an organized time for questions and answers after the kickoff. *The biggest mistake:* You don't plan enough. You can't wing it. Set the proper framing for the meeting, as well as a structured agenda. If you have other speakers, they *must* be in sync with the approach.

- *All-company meetings. Approach:* It should be similar to that for a keynote presentation, but with more specific answers. *Audience:* At the company meeting, employees are often looking for an inspirational speech with solid information. If you are delivering bad news, be empathetic, show your emotion, and take your time. *The biggest mistake:* Now what? You don't invite your listeners to use what they've just learned. End with positive and inspirational action items.

- *Marketing presentations.* *Approach:* This depends on the audience, but if it is to consumers, then appeal to their emotions, including stories and examples. *Audience:* If it's consumers, be ready to be interrupted. If it's top executives, also be prepared to be interrupted. As with a sales or update presentation, love the interruptions. *The biggest mistake:* You do the same presentation no matter what the audience.
- *Venture capital presentations.* *Approach:* You hope these listeners will finance you. It should be deductive and inspirational, and should use less time than you are given, leaving plenty of room for questions. (Venture capitalists listen to presentations all day—too many of them bad.) Find the balance between emotion and logic in your content and delivery. If your strength is logic and not emotion, use a teammate to kick up the pathos. *Audience:* Expect to be interrupted as you go and prepare to jump from one section of your talk to another with ease. *The biggest mistake:* Besides going on too long, you don't keep track of all the components that must be conveyed before the presentation ends.
- *Presentations when you want active participation from your listeners.* *Approach:* It should be conversational and instructional. For example, if you want to see a show of hands, raise your hand and say, "Give me a show of hands from people who . . ." *Audience:* Expect to be challenged, and be prepared to say, "I don't know, and I look forward to getting back to you by the end of the day." *The biggest mistake:* You let someone take over the presentation. When someone talks too much or too long, find a pause in his monologue and say, "Tom, that's great thinking, and let me hear from Jim or Carrie, too."

The Basics

Visuals

A visual aid is just that. It's to aid you. It's not the presentation. *You* are the presentation. You are not a human aid to the visuals. In the business world, people have learned to think through PowerPoint. The problem is that people write all their thoughts on PowerPoint and then throw them up 10 feet high or take over the whole screen on a virtual presentation. On the same note, in most business presentations you usually can't just have a deck full of photographs.

In your daily business communications where you're updating the vice president on your progress, do you actually need visual aids? What will your visuals emphasize? We'd rather have you outline your presentation first, before you put the PowerPoint together. Too often when people put their bullet points on a slide, they make them all sentences and expect the audience members to read them from a slide. This problem is plaguing visual aids throughout the work world.

Visuals are not just slides. They include your hands and anything you hold up, and there are three simple guidelines:

1. *Be synchronized.* People shouldn't see it until you say it. You have to say everything that's on the slide. You're saying right now, "Oh, no. That's so boring." Exactly. If it's boring to read everything that's on the screen, change your visual. Should your listeners be reading or listening to you? Try to read an email while someone's talking to you. It's not easy. When you're out of sync, you're making them choose. You become technically boring. Your listeners will read faster than you can talk. You're talking about point number one, but they've read through number six, and now they don't need you.

   So use short bullet points—either a single word or a brief phrase. What takes longer to present, one slide with six bullet points, or six slides with one bullet point each? What's heavier, a ton of bricks or a ton of feathers? They take the same amount of time to present, but one is synchronized and the other is not. People say, "My deck already has 73 slides. I can't add more." The number of slides is irrelevant. We hear terms like "death by PowerPoint" because presenters have busy slides and start talking one bullet point at a time. It becomes physically difficult for the listeners to pay attention.

Synchronization is different in virtual presentations. Don't start with slides. If you have a title slide up while people are gathering, take it down before you begin speaking. Because the slide consumes most of the screen, people can't appreciate your nonverbal communication. They need to experience you before a slide will be most valuable. Begin with what you are going to tell them and why it matters. Then use slides to emphasize the points you want to make. Turn off screen sharing when you aren't using slides for a period of time because your audience needs to see you as much as possible to build a connection. Always finish with you talking without slides. The last thing you want people to remember is you delivering the clear point of the presentation.

2. *Introduction and setup.* If what a slide shows is text, click the button when you get to the word. If it's a graph, describe to your listeners what they're about to see before you click. For example, here's your introduction: "As we talk about the numbers from the last year, I'm going to show you a graph that maps our progress for the last four quarters." Then you give the setup: "What I want you to look at is Q4, on the left side of the screen, which I've circled in red." Then you click. The setup gives the visual specifics of what you want your listeners to look at. It guarantees that every one of them is looking at the part of the graph you want them to look at. If you don't introduce and set up a graph or chart, they will be looking at the screen and trying to figure it out for themselves. They'll no longer be paying attention to you.

3. *Talk and do.* If you're an architect setting up your model, a teacher writing on the board, or a minister pouring wine, your ability to talk while you do things is often the difference between visuals that work and those that distract. Don't write on a whiteboard slowly, one letter at a time, after you tell them what you're going to talk about. In the computer world, if you're doing a demo, don't sit there in silence while your computer is rebooting. Clear everything off your desktop

except the application you're using. When the computer does restart, you can then start again easily instead of having people stare at you anxiously while you look at your computer and say, "It's here somewhere." In the virtual world, talk as you share your screen. Radio silence disrupts appreciation of your message.

Identify Key Words or Terms

Choose the key words and terms that emphasize your point, and then reread Chapter 6 on adding color.

How Do I Calm My Nerves?

You may never overcome nervousness, but that's okay. Nervousness is not the problem for most people. In many cases, you can use nervous energy to strengthen your delivery. You can learn to control it. What is technically referred to as the "fear of public speaking" is commonly known as one of the top three fears in the United States and is worse outside of the United States. So, if you feel nervous, know that you're not alone.

This fear is so common because public speaking affects people differently. One speaker can stand in front of 1,000 people at a conference and feel comfortable but will feel very nervous speaking in front of the Board or giving a wedding toast. Another speaker will have a completely opposite response to the same environments.

There are two areas that you can focus on to make you feel more comfortable: the physiological and the psychological. Physically, the body is prewired to react when faced with fear. We take in air differently. We go from diaphragmatic breathing, which is used in yoga when we are in a relaxed state, talking, or singing, to upper thoracic breathing, which is how we breathe when we are running or working out. This is done to create pressure that will be released for upper body strength. Upper thoracic breathing is great when we need to punch, run, or lift, because we release that extra pressure in our movements.

When we are doing public speaking and are faced with fear, we don't release that pressure. As a result it comes out in other ways, like shaky hands, a quivering voice, turning red, or losing our train of thought.

Here are two techniques to stop it:

1. ***Learn to breath diaphragmatically.*** Control your breathing. Stand straight up, take a deep breath in, then, as you exhale, count out loud, saying, "1 by 1 and 2 by 2 and 3 by 3," and so on until you reach 20. When you run out of breath, stop. The number you stopped on represents the strength of your diaphragm. When you can get to 20 comfortably, push your number to 30. Make sure to do this in front of a mirror while wearing a tight shirt. The goal is to breathe using your diaphragm, the area below your ribs that looks like your stomach when you fill it with air, and not your chest. When we work with professional athletes, they have a tough time with this because they are trained to breath upper thoracically most of the time.

2. ***Focus the energy.*** Hold your index finger and thumb together, press as hard as you can for 10 seconds, and then let go. This creates a pressure point in your body that will redirect the nervous energy so that it goes to your fingers, instead of to your brain or red cheeks. Repeat as needed.

If you want to deal with the psychological aspect of public speaking, you have to change what you believe about speaking. There are many spectacularly goofy devices that people will offer as advice, like the famous "visualize them in their underwear." Instead, for true and sustainable change in your nervousness, identify what you believe about that speaking situation and change it.

For instance, if you believe a deal and your livelihood is dependent on a presentation, you will feel nerves. You should feel nerves. The belief "I must win the deal or I will lose my job" has to change to "I love presenting on this topic I know so well." Turn the false statement of the talk's risk into a simple goal or purpose that you know you can live out. "Impress one person" or "Teach each person one new thing" are examples of goals. "Communicate value" or "Introduce a new idea" are examples of purpose. You may need to write down the new belief about what the presentation means.

Your clarity about why you are presenting is so important because this is not a theatrical approach. You are not an actor. Unless you are, in which case you should use what you've learned that works for you. But know that your people don't have the kind of time needed to learn acting technique. Theatrical-based approaches for overcoming things like "stage fright" are different. An actor may be brilliant on screen but a nervous wreck at the award shows.

At work, you're not being paid to pretend or to act like a leader. Your presentation has to be your style for a reason that is true to you. Don't be afraid to use therapists, coaches, or trusted advisors to help. There's rarely an over-the-weekend fix. But with time and practice, you can learn to control the anxiety. You may even find yourself looking for opportunities to speak in public.

How Innovation Begins with Presentation: Jeanette Horan

Jeanette Horan, a Board member at Wolters Kluwer NV and Nokia, was vice president of enterprise business transformation, part of IBM's internal CIO office. She was responsible for a global transformation program for the entire company. As she described the business at the time of change:

> My work was about the way IBM does business. We grew up as a hardware company, but now 50 percent of our revenue was from services and 40 percent of our profits were from software. The company was trying to go to market as a globally integrated enterprise, so we wanted common processes across the world so that we could go to market with integrated solutions of software, hardware, and services. Our internal IT systems were inhibitors to our being able to do that. It was about simplifying how we take orders, process orders, deliver products, and manage our books.

Her direct staff was less than 20, but she had 600 people working on the project. She presented to audiences around the world, from small internal groups to external audiences of five or ten thousand. She didn't like presenting at first: "The first time I had to give a presentation, I was scared stiff, and it comes through in the way you present. Then I got to the point where I was very comfortable presenting in a relatively small setting. It came from knowing my material. I was the subject matter expert, and I was confident that I knew what I was talking about." Now she wins awards for her large presentations.

But leaders and managers become masters in front of large audiences by giving effective presentations to a few people. Horan grew up in the United Kingdom, went to the University of London, earned a math degree, and started working in technology. She immediately ran into bad presentations. "A lot of the brilliant technical people make terrible people managers. They lack self-awareness. They don't think about or understand how their style is perceived by others. If you have opportunities to understand how others perceive you, and you listen and take the feedback, you can modify your style in different situations. There's no one style that is effective in every situation, so you need to think about how you can modify your style to get different results." She took feedback and practiced. Horan said that:

I've always done very well in an interactive dialogue; maybe I'm giving a formal presentation, but there are questions and answers along the way. But standing up and giving a speech has been the most difficult for me, and particularly in a very, very large environment with five to ten thousand people in the room and the lights and the stage. It's very scary because you are up there alone.

Her skill came from repetition, she said:

It's practice. It's getting that confidence that nothing bad is going to happen. The floor is not going to open up and swallow you. You're not going to trip and fall. This is really like having a dialogue with someone in a smaller room, but there are 5,000 others listening. A couple of things have really helped. Knowing the subject. Knowing the audience: What is its context? Why are people listening? Knowing the setting. When I'm giving a presentation, I want to know: Where is the projector? How do I advance the charts? I want to know the physical environment so that I'm not worried about those things.

When it comes to message, it's about focus. "What is the message in 10 words or less?" Do you know how hard it is for a lot of people to get the theme statement into 10 words or less? I had a lot of people who prepared material for me, and as we sat down, I asked, "What's the storyboard? How does this relate to what we're talking about?" I get very picky about the order of things because it has to fit my story. Everything is a story, and it has the theme statement, and it helps you to stay focused. There's nothing worse than someone meandering around the subject.

IBM even uses technology to spread presentations and rate the success of a presentation, related Horan:

We were 380,000 employees. You have a global project, so how do you connect? We used podcasts. We used to use teleconferences, but the one thing you can't control is time zones. So we would record something in a group setting, but then it gets published as a podcast so that people can listen on their own time. I knew I had an impact based on the number of emails I got. I knew I was successful based on how many teams ask me to talk to their team.

In the modern world, a great presentation can live forever and build your ethos inside and outside of your company.

How TED Tells a Story: June Cohen

TED meets each year in Monterey, California. It started in 1984 as a conference celebrating the convergence between technology, entertainment, and design. For years the conference was invitation-only, the audience was 1,000 of the smartest people in the world, and the twist was that presenters had 18 minutes each. Over time, the speakers have expanded across disciplines to include public figures like Bill Clinton, business giants like Richard Branson and Bill Gates, and scientists like

Jane Goodall. One thing hasn't changed: they each get 18 minutes. In 2020, TED talks will have been viewed online over 11 billion times, so not only are presenters in front of the world's most impressive audience, but their talks truly become permanently accessible to the world. If you learn what TED speakers do to excel under this incredible pressure, you can master any presentation.

TED's long-time executive producer from 2004–2015, June Cohen, explained why people are flocking to view the presentations online: "TED captures the zeitgeist of the moment. It speaks to people's higher goals. We're at a moment in our country and in the world when people need inspiration, a sense of optimism; they want to have a sense that there is a higher purpose that they can work toward, and TED is fueling this."

In your organization, you will rarely give a TED talk—an inspirational, keynote-style presentation. You probably won't tell your team a story about how you came to love computer programming as a child when you're doing a weekly update on the bugs you need to fix in your new product. But can you make even the presentation of your weekly update to your team more significant than just giving the numbers?

What makes a TED talk great can make you a great presenter in any arena. Cohen clarified:

A great TED talk tells a story. It doesn't just deliver facts. It is personal and a little bit vulnerable—it reveals a little something about the speaker that moves the audience. It is mind-opening, a new angle on looking at the world. It uses humor as a way to open people's hearts and teach them things that they didn't know. It's bigger than it seems, and it draws on a higher purpose. Even if you're talking about a scientific discovery or product, it has a meaning beyond the immediate topic. It's rehearsed, but the audience doesn't know it, and it comes in at under 18 minutes.

You can be a better presenter than you ever imagined. Cohen said:

There's an incredible, unacknowledged power in a single person passionately conveying an idea. It's the most ancient form of media: Someone standing up and telling you a story and either persuading you of an idea, or communicating what they've learned, or just inspiring you. When you're watching a compelling speaker, it affects you, not just on an intellectual level, but on an emotional level, and I'd argue a chemical level. When you watch people watching an inspired speaker, it's almost as if they're in a trance; they're almost hypnotized by her; they're being taken on a journey.

People are doing this at work. "You can find it within some great companies," Cohen explained. "People are hungry for the kind of inspiration they get from a leader when he stands up, tells a story, and aims to inspire, and we just don't get enough of this in our modern lives. We don't have a lot of opportunities to be inspired by great leaders and thinkers."

You can prepare like you're presenting at TED. Cohen mentioned that:

We explained to presenters that 18 minutes is exactly the right amount of time. It's long enough to develop a point, but short enough to keep everybody involved and interested. We encouraged them to focus in on their central story. They can't pack everything they've ever done into 18 minutes, and they will give a much stronger presentation once they've distilled it down.

On a tactical level, we encouraged them to really think about what they want people to feel, to learn, and to do. What are the "Aha!" moments they want people to have? We had them rehearse. I told this to every speaker, no matter how experienced she was. You have to make sure you can fit it into 18 minutes. Ideally, you'll have to run through it five times with people listening or actual audiences. Even very experienced speakers prepare well ahead of time. The stakes for a TED Talk became really high. It made people crazy with nerves.

And, Cohen said, TED presenters are at risk of making the same mistakes with slides that plague presenters at work:

One of the biggest mistakes people made at TED and elsewhere was conveying too much information on the slides. Speakers used the slides as a crutch or wanted people to read them as an outline while they were talking. It was probably the number one problem we saw. Now, data-driven slides are expected in boardrooms and in scientific meetings. But the vast majority of presentations don't require that level of detail. Persuading people isn't about presenting them with more data, it's about telling them a story.

How Do You Know the Format Worked?

People remember. They remember your point, your stories, or your data. If it's the kind of presentation where you need them to act, they know what they need to do. The best presentations are not the flashiest, where you fill up all the time allotted and everyone thinks you're a great speaker. In organizations, if you are the leader or the manager, you tailor your content to the context. You have a clear message. Whatever the goal of your presentation is, you achieve it.

CHAPTER 12

HIRING INTERVIEWS

Hiring is finding the right people for your team. It is the bridge between your culture today and a more communicative, effective culture in the future. Too often, leaders and managers get stuck in generic, preprogrammed interviews and hire the wrong person. In this chapter, you will learn how to discover the information you need if you are to make smart hiring decisions.

The Sixth Moment: Hiring Interviews

Hire poorly, and you will create horror stories of wasted time and frustrated colleagues. Hire the right person and he will produce results exponentially larger than the investment you make in him. The right person is clearer than you think, and the story of finding him begins with the interview. The moment that matters in hiring is the interview. Effective interviewing takes preparation and a plan.

Too often, the pressured environment of meeting with you prevents candidates from clearly articulating their skills and accurately portraying who they are. As a result, you might find that their technical ability is strong, but you are turned off by who they seem to be as a person. We're going to talk about how, in some cases, you intentionally create extra stress because you want to see how candidates will react. In general, however, your job is to foster a comfortable experience so that the candidate can open up. The result: you'll have higher-quality information from which to assess this person's fit with your team.

The Trap

You don't know what you need. Many managers fall into the trap of focusing on the technical side of a position. They either forget or don't know how to reveal the person's character and talent. In addition to finding a person who can execute the functions of the position, you need a teammate. You need someone whom your colleagues will be really happy to work with and who will make everyone's lives better.

What you need has a context, too. Your culture is unique. You need to know its idiosyncrasies, its expectations, and the characteristics a person must embrace to become a valuable contributor in your world. If you're not familiar with your organization's culture, how can you figure out if someone is a fit? You need to be able to portray with laser precision the challenges that make the job you want her to do worth spending 40 to 100 hours a week doing. If you can't, you may end up hiring someone who understands the technology or the tasks of the job but brings down morale or creates tension on your team. Now you are stuck with the challenge of letting the person go, not to mention the time and money wasted on the wrong person.

The Format

1. *Make candidates comfortable.* If they are uncomfortable, they will put on their game face. In fact, they'll have their interview mask on from the beginning. If they stay in that mode, they are acting. People begin interviews on their best behavior, and that's dangerous for you. You need to know how they will behave on a regular day. If you notice that someone is nervous, find ways to help him settle into the conversation. Be intentional about where you sit. Don't sit behind your desk. Don't sit across a conference table. Physical barriers

feel distant. Find the natural place where the candidate can be himself, so that the two of you can discover whether your relationship has potential.

For virtual interviews, the person may already be comfortable as they talk with you from their home. But interruptions are more likely to happen. Your ease when someone in their family pops onto their screen or the dog starts barking will help the person relax and be natural. Make sure you can hear each other clearly at the beginning because they might not mention it if your connection is poor. A good connection is essential to a meaningful conversation.

2. *Frame the interview.* Just as you would frame a meeting, frame this conversation. Let the candidate know how long the conversation will last and what you want to explore with him. Then ask your first question, which you've prepared ahead of time. It should be about the candidate. It should not be a difficult question. In fact, it should be so simple that it reveals whether he is comfortable or not.

3. *Be quiet.* This is perhaps the most important reminder we can offer—stop talking. The biggest mistake that interviewers make is talking too much. You listen so much of the day, and here is a person who has to listen to you. He wants the job, so he will let you keep talking. The result can be that you didn't listen long enough to judge who he really is. If he is able to interject when you are talking and redirect the conversation to continue the process of gathering and giving information, then you have a sign that he is a skilled communicator. If he does this but he offends you, it also tells you something important about his ability to build relationships.

4. *Explore fit.* Fit is about intention, capability, the stage of your business, hierarchy, and communication tendencies. This is the core of the interview (more about this in the next section).

5. *Detail your expectations.* Even if the candidate seems to be a good fit, you want your expectations to be as clear as a cloudless day. You need to write down what you expect this person to do. If you expect him to work at two in the morning

on weekends, you need to make it explicit that this could happen. You need to give examples like "When we go to conferences in Las Vegas, we could be working until two in the morning. Tell me why that works for you." It can be very difficult to change expectations after the person is hired. Come to the interview prepared to paint what you feel is the most challenging or potentially challenging part of the position. Then gauge his comfort level through his response.

6. *Be clear about the next steps.* At the end of the interview, let the candidate know what happens next. If he is a good fit, you've already set the expectation about how you end meetings and how you'll want him to communicate. But don't let him leave until you've said, "So, to make sure I was clear, tell me what's going to happen next." The answer gives more evidence about his talent.

Is the Person a Good Fit?

Fit is so much bigger than personality type. You might love this person if you met him at your child's soccer game, but when you add the stress of work and all the elements that contribute to your environment, it might not work. Fit is bigger than just work style. Fit is about how the person's work style will contribute to where your business is today, the model of leadership you practice, and how you expect people to communicate. You have to explore fit in the interview. If the fit is right, when you ask specific questions, the answers will feel right to you. The person's comfort and excitement will show you that what you're talking about works for him. In exploring fit, start with the following:

> *Intention.* You want to figure out what he really wants. Why is he interviewing? Is he really interested in making a difference in your organization, or does he just need a job? Does he want to climb up the political ladder? Understanding the intention will help you determine his motivation once he's on your team.

Capabilities. You know what's on the candidate's résumé, but that's only a start. You have to hear him describe how he has managed different situations in order to assess the quality of his capabilities. You want to hear firsthand how the person might handle a given situation. You don't just want to know that he was a manager in a different company or that he worked with a particular technology or performed a skill. You want to know how he thinks. How does he handle conflict? How will he handle the unique challenges of the job?

In an interview, you get this level of clarity by encouraging the candidate to tell stories. If he's well trained, he'll already tell stories. Say, "Tell me a story about how you dealt with a difficult customer." Ask, "What did you do the last time a person at work made you angry?" You may need to customize the questions for your situation. Have the candidate share narratives of the real work you want him to do and notice whether his answers match your culture.

The stage of your business. If you are a start-up with three employees and you expect people to work 60 to 80 hours a week, that's very different from a corporation that's been in business for a hundred years, has 20,000 employees, and keeps regular hours. You want to ask, "Tell me about the culture of the last business where you worked." The person may be excited about making a change, but you need to know that it will be a shock to his system. A start-up junkie coming into an established business will get really frustrated when everyone goes home at five. A person who has logged 40 to 50 hours a week and had summer hours for seven years will almost certainly choke on your request that he do an all-nighter.

Hierarchy. Does the person need structure? Is he used to structure? To figure this out, have him describe the environment in which he was most effective. Some companies are flat. Digi, one of the leading mobile phone providers in Southeast Asia, has no offices and no assigned cubicles. With thousands of employees, it's a first-come, first-served basis every day at the office. This was designed to create a truly flat organization. That won't work for every candidate. In flat companies, everyone is expected to contribute. Everyone's opinion is equally valued. People joke and tease the CEO and get heated in meetings when they disagree with her idea (not at her, but at her idea if the company is doing it right). In other organizations, there is a strict sense of hierarchy. The ladder is clear. If you are lower, you do what the person above you says. Your company has a structure: will it grate on this candidate, or will she fit in naturally?

Communication tendencies. Is your team inductive or deductive? Are most of its members internal or external? If you bring an inductive, external thinker onto a team of deductive, internal computer programmers who meet for 10 minutes a week and keep their headphones on all day, the person will go crazy. The team members won't notice because they're jamming to their favorite tunes. You may want to change the mix of your team on purpose, but you need to communicate this in the interview so that the person knows why he is being hired. He needs to describe how he will handle the inevitable challenges of being the change agent.

Attitude, Round Two

Listen for the person's vocabulary and tone. Attitude creates defensiveness. It also helps determine fit. It is a separate category because if you believe that someone is a good fit, then you want to understand that person's belief about your company, what you do, and why you do it. At a computer company where the environment is young and hip, the style is funky, and the attitude is "We have this kick-ass product and a loyal group of followers," the culture vibrates with that belief. Does the person you're interviewing match it?

In a financial firm that is serious and sophisticated, the attitude may be "We are number one because we are intellectuals." Consider the attitude of a young, rebellious skateboarder, even if he had a 4.0 average, majored in finance, and put on a suit for the interview. If you posed him a scenario about how he'd approach a client who wants to adjust her portfolio, and his response is, "I'd say, 'What's up? Let's talk about it,'" you have to be comfortable with that response. The skill here for the master communicator is to go into the interview knowing what you need the candidate's attitude to be. Get this right, as attitudes are very difficult to change.

Someone you hire could easily start offending the best performers in your office because he has a different attitude about the work. He may have that attitude on purpose, and it isn't wrong. It just may not be right for your office. The same problem can arise when a young, rebellious skateboard company decides that it needs to grow up, so it hires a suit. If you bring in someone who has an attitude that is not a match, it will be virtually impossible to change it. Your teammates might say, "What's wrong with him? He's so uptight." Unless everyone agrees that you want to change the culture, that you want someone with a different attitude to help you do that, it's a bad fit.

How do you recognize attitude? It's in a person's face, choice of words, and the way the person speaks. Notice how he adds color. People have been trained to dress up in a suit and tie and not show their true self in a job interview. Have the candidate walk with you on the manufacturing floor or around your office. See how he interacts with your people. To frame what you're doing, don't say, "Let me see how you look in the manufacturing environment." Say, "Hey, let's go take a walk." Introduce the candidate to certain people to see if the attitudes are compatible. Just because two people don't have a lot to say doesn't mean that they won't fit. But if the attitude fits, you'll see each person relax.

How to Perform the Interview They Least Expect: Jason Hanold

Jason Hanold is an expert at helping professionals discover what they do best. Leading as a partner and managing director at Russell Reynolds

Associates, one of the big five executive search firms, and now as owner of Hanold Associates, he places executives at companies where their leadership style and personality match the culture.

As he assesses chief HR and corporate officers, his gift is in making people comfortable and asking the questions that help them be honest. "There are interviewers who try to trip up the candidate," says Hanold. "If you make people do intellectual gymnastics, you're not getting their true self. There is no right answer to any question I ask. I want an authentic response."

To understand a candidate's attitude and character, he focuses on who the person is:

> I always ask at the very beginning: "Tell me about your mother and father and the environment in which you were raised. What attributes do you bring forward?" The questions are very personal, but the harder the answers are to talk about, the more influence they've had on the person's being. If Dad was never there, that will affect the person today, and his work-life balance will be more important. I'd never put that person with a CEO who works every Saturday and Sunday. It has nothing to do with job qualifications, but it has everything to do with how someone performs and getting people into the right culture where they will stick and thrive.

Hanold began learning the skills he uses at work every day when he was growing up. As an only child whose mom was an emergency room nurse working nights and weekends, he was often shipped off to different relatives. "When you spend a lot of time at the homes of extended family," observes Hanold, "you learn how to make yourself welcome. I always had to have a high level of adaptability, and that translated into a curiosity about what motivates and drives people."

He's used that skill throughout his career:

> I started in Auto Claims with State Farm Insurance. When you're speaking with a surviving spouse, and all you can do is write a check, it becomes about the tragedies and realities of everyday life. In Claims they taught me not what you can deny, but to look for ways to pay claims

because everyone is a potential policyholder. In reconstructing claims, you may detect fraud. This was my first experience with interviewing people and discovering what really happened.

This natural ability led to a new career in recruitment. "My management team noticed my ability to draw details out of people," notes Hanold. "They said, 'You help people feel comfortable, and they talk to you. They want to share things with you.' It allowed us to resolve claims very quickly."

Hanold took his curiosity and capacity for making people comfortable into roles as director of recruiting at McKinsey & Company in New York, Americas director for executive recruiting at Deloitte Consulting, and head of global talent at Whirlpool Corporation, a company of 70,000, where he was responsible for raising the assessment capability of the organization.

His format for interviews allows him to understand the culture in which the executives he serves will succeed. He begins by setting context:

I rarely dive in and say, "Tell me about yourself." I start with sharing on both sides—about someone's background, about the role, and about the purpose of the interview. Then I ask people about their current situation. Their answers give me a way of framing their motivation, and by understanding their mindset, I can better understand their purpose and what they are trying to achieve through our conversation.

Then I'm mindful of the hierarchy of needs and fostering an environment for sharing. First, I have to create a safe environment where you can speak confidentially, and a platform for trust is established.

Second, I want to create emotional resonance. People think of interviews as evaluations and constant judgment. I listen without judging. I have incredibly unreliable first impressions, and I've proved myself wrong too often. If you reserve judgment until the end of the conversation and you don't express an opinion in your tone and body language, that creates resonance.

Third, we share stories about our lives. What draws you or me to a leader is sharing common attributes. You are a person with interests, and people with shared interests resonate with one another. It's when your integrity aligns. You could have the same skill, but if the other person doesn't have the same integrity, you won't be drawn to him."

Notice how Hanold has said, "We share." An interview is not a one-way exchange. It's about gathering and giving information. His attitude is set in a way that will naturally foster a collaborative experience, which will enable the candidate to feel comfortable almost immediately:

> Last, if you can leave something with the candidate that will confirm that you truly heard her, you validate the honest exchange of information. When you offer nonjudgmental counsel or a simple observation that she may not have otherwise considered, she leaves the interview having gained something.

As you share stories, you ask questions that reveal the true nature of the candidate. Because Hanold places chief HR officers who interview others for a living, his questions are intentional and nuanced. He says that:

> HR officers know their themes, their strengths and weaknesses, so I ask questions like, "Tell me about misconceptions about you." That way, they can help me correct my own judgments and show me where they've had trouble in the past.
>
> Then I go into personal effectiveness interviewing. I ask the person to explore a situation in which he was successful. Now I can ask what he did. What was he thinking? It brings to life a real situation. Since the answers aren't rehearsed, this pulls from the person's well of truth and gets at his authentic behaviors, such as how collaborative he is and whether he is effective at essential activities like delegating.

But knowing whether the interview delved into the true character of the other person is the biggest challenge. Asserts Hanold:

> To know if I'm successful, I read the person's body language and eye contact, and listen to what she says as we're concluding. I want people to say, "Although we had an interview, it didn't feel like an interview."

When you start interviewing people, they fall into the role of candidate. People commonly revert to business speak. I don't want people to fall into a role; I want them to be themselves.

And Hanold prefers to ask introspective questions outside the office. "Some of the best interviews are over dinner. That's when the dimensions and colors emerge. I want to interview people at the end of the day, when the individual has nowhere else to be." He loves his work because he facilitates bettering someone else's position in life: "It's humbling, and it's such a responsibility: to this person, you have an impact on her world. By what she shares, she empowers you to make a difference for her." If your purpose in interviewing a candidate is to discover her true capacity to help an organization, then your conversation will uncover the work she loves to do and whether your organization is an environment in which she can succeed.

Sometimes You Are the Candidate

You Need to Get Hired

The average life of an employee in an organization used to be 20 years or more. Then in the 1990s, the average dropped to around five years, then to two. As the average goes up and down, you will almost certainly work for more than one organization in the course of your career. If you can learn what a well-prepared candidate does to interview like a master, you'll know what to look for when you're hiring. You'll also be ready the next time you need a job.

Prepared Candidates Have a Theme

In a formal presentation, *theme* is a technical term. It's a clear declarative statement, usually less than 10 words. In an interview, the theme is not a declarative statement. It is the main idea that you want your interviewer to remember about you after the conversation. You need two of them: a personal theme and a professional theme.

For example, if you're a manager of engineers, your personal theme might be that you're competitive, and your professional theme might be that you create an environment in which people beat deadlines. The actual themes you choose may vary based on the specific position you're interviewing for. Be prepared with examples that demonstrate why both themes are true for you.

When you're interviewing a candidate, can you identify his personal and professional themes?

Sell Yourself

For people who are not in sales, selling yourself is a foreign concept. You have a brief interaction to generate interest in you as the right person for the role. The interviewer can't read your mind. You need to be clear and promote the idea that you can do the job. You can't act. Positioning why you will add value to the organization has to be natural. Here is an outline that ensures that you will sell yourself in any interviewing environment. How you implement it comes from your style and creativity:

1. *A can-do statement.* You need to indicate that you can actually do this job. Don't assume that because the interviewer sees your experience on the résumé, she will connect the dots. You have to verbalize it. Remind the interviewer that your experience makes you qualified for this job. For example, when you interview for an engineering position at an aerospace company, you might say: "One of the reasons I'm here today is designing airplanes is what I love to do."

2. *The benefit you offer.* How will you benefit the team? This is the toughest part for non-sales pros. A helpful way to place a check next to this one is to ask the interviewer. For example, "Tom, as you look over my background, how do you see me fitting into the team?" Now you'll have him telling you how he sees you benefiting him.

3. *Experience.* This is your résumé, and it got you the interview. To strengthen the interviewer's impression of what you've done before, be prepared to tell stories about your experiences.

4. *Your work style.* This is a critical step. You need to have dialogue about what it's like to work there and how you like to

work. For example, do people go out after work? Is it a serious or a fun environment? Talk about the details to see if the culture is a good fit for your lifestyle.

5. *The next action.* What happens next? You might ask if there is a time frame for making a decision or at least seek clarification concerning the next steps. Propose to send something as a follow-up. Don't leave the interview until you know the next step in the process.

Preparation doesn't mean a canned interview. These are the areas that you should be prepared to talk about with fluency. If you're the interviewer, and the answers start coming out like a prepared speech, ask the candidate to tell stories. Then challenge him with questions based on those stories, such as: Why did you make that choice? What was your thought process? How would you do it differently next time? You want candidates who are prepared because that's how they will work in your organization. You want leaders who can improvise with what they know. Going on an interview, be ready to do both. In an interview, test for both.

Not the Usual Interview

Group Interviews

Group or panel interviews are rarely the most effective way to determine if someone is a fit for your team. Panel interviews intimidate even the best candidates, and that puts them back on their best behavior. But you already know how candidates behave when they are formal. That is how they first greeted you and communicated with you in the first interview. Their comfort reveals their true character. It's difficult to create a group experience where a candidate won't be trying to please at least someone in the group.

If you do choose to do a panel interview, be strategic. Choose a moderator to keep the conversation focused. Give each person a specific area around which to concentrate his questions. It's best to avoid putting the candidate on a folding chair in the center of a room, with a light shining on his face and your team in a circle around him—unless you've found that the hostile, you-versus-them technique works in finding the best talent. A better panel setting is sitting around a conference table so that the person feels like part of the team. It gives the best chance of helping him relax and the clearest window into how he would handle a meeting.

When to Create a Stressful Interview

There are unique strategies for interviewing people for specific types of jobs. In the first interview, you want the person to be comfortable—that is, to get through his nerves and his interview mask. If you think that someone is a good fit, but you are interviewing him for a stressful job or your work environment has unique pressures, you need to expose him to those stresses. In fact, you want to make him profoundly uncomfortable and see how he performs.

For instance, when an analyst is taken seriously enough that you might make him an offer, you want to put him in front of the other analysts. Whatever the field, if this person is going to be dealing with hypercritical clients or customers, you may want to create an environment that will demonstrate how he handles himself under pressure. For example, you might set up a meeting with an abrasive colleague or create an intentionally awkward meeting where teammates contradict everything he says.

Make sure you plan this out. If done poorly, it will appear unprofessional. You don't have to trick the person or catch him off guard. Before the next interview tell him, "When we have you come back, we are going to set up some difficult conversations that simulate the challenges of this job."

How Do You Know the Format Worked?

Other people are excited. If they aren't, get worried. The whole point of hiring is to make your work lives better. When an interview process has produced a candidate that your team wants to work with, when your team members believe that you have just given them another resource, their morale lifts. Their excitement is based on their interaction with the candidate and, perhaps most importantly, your ability to describe him. If you can validate the specific value that he will offer the team, both the pain that he will take away and the new insights and talent that he brings, you give him ethos. When you've followed the format of the interview, he'll have no trouble keeping that ethos.

SECTION 3

A CULTURE OF COMMUNICATION

Mastering Communication at Work, from Home: An Introduction to Section 3

The world will never work the same way again. In 2020, the global health crisis changed the way we think about productive communication. Almost overnight, organizations that believed dogmatically in offices and traveling for face-to-face meetings were forced to embrace virtual meetings and conversations. Virtual communication, it turns out, can be an impactful form of meaningful interaction. Many jobs can be done better away from the office. A portion of every organization—whether based on introversion, less distractions at home, or the removal of a commute—loves virtual work. As a result, for some people at least some of the time, virtual communication will always be part of the future workplace.

Additionally, for another segment of every organization—extraverts, families without enough space or singles with roommates, and thinkers who need people and diverse environments to be creative and effective—virtual communication is a nightmare. No matter how useful videoconferencing software becomes, humans were not made to sit in one place in front of a computer screen all day. The blue light confuses our circadian rhythms. The lack of movement steals our focus. Meeting after meeting after meeting without a break simply causes cognitive fatigue. But the efficiency and ease of gathering people virtually means we have to build best practices for communicating in the virtual environment to create an effective culture of communication.

Virtual interaction is not the same as communicating in person. Mastering communication in the virtual world and folding it into the permanent workflow still starts with the skills and moments from the first 12 chapters. What's different is the way you send messages. On a daily basis, you need to invent new reasons to interact that make up for the micro-interactions that go away when we are not physically together. Relationships that used to be built with casual conversation over meals now also need a different forum. Organizations that met yearly, at great expense, can now, at a fraction of the cost, virtually gather thousands at a time every quarter. But people knew how to absorb information in the conference setting. What are the signs and symbols of a cravable virtual conference?

To lead, manage, and influence, you have to notice and adjust for the subtle difference between communicating in voice and 2D versus live in-person interaction. Presentations, handouts or agendas, and demonstrations now need to become texts, chats, blogs, and podcasts. Events, at least some of the time, will be more like watching live TV. Just knowing how to use the latest technology is not enough either. You have to prepare your ethos in a new world where the rules are still being defined.

Should I meet in person or is virtual appropriate? When is voice enough? When should I be on camera? Can my dog enter the screen? What if my kids need me during a meeting? Is putting comments in the chat during a virtual event helpful or distracting? When do I use slides? Where should I be looking so I seem engaged? The new culture of communication is both virtual and in person. Master communicators value the opportunities to connect in both arenas.

CHAPTER 13

VIRTUAL COMMUNICATION

Technology Drives New Forms of Communication

If you look at the technology curve for computers, a significant increase in the speed of hardware led to an increased adoption of the personal computer. The computer was the disruptor changing the way people worked, and then, how they communicated. Face-to-face meetings, telephone calls, and letters were joined by electronic mail, and the world has not looked back. The smartphone added texting and social media. The ubiquity of tablets and laptops, the cloud, and high-definition quality video added videoconferencing. People can connect from anywhere in the world almost like we are in the same room.

The technology drives new forms of communication and the new frontier of building a communication culture. But now the challenges are more complex than just effectively sharing messages, giving feedback, and making decisions. When there are so many forms of communication, which one works best for which interaction? Virtual communication is not the same as being in the same room, and certain signals and patterns that create connection are lost. What are the best practices of the virtual world?

The attention needed to communicate virtually demands the vision of a television director and the flexibility of a third-grade teacher. Virtual communication uses a different set of signs and symbols. In person, you can smell stress. In person, you pick up on nonverbal cues that reveal whether a gathering is going well or not. In the virtual world, sight and sound are all we have. What we hear, or can't hear, and what we see transmit the message.

Even experienced virtual communicators are still new to the discipline of leading entire teams virtually. The leader in the virtual world has to deal with precocious experts and struggling enthusiasts who all want to be successful. Success in virtual communication and building a culture that includes impactful virtual interaction begins with understanding the nuances between settings. Successful virtual communication happens when every member of your team embraces clear expectations of how to take advantage of the new world.

Differentiating the Virtual and the 3D World

Micro-Interactions Have to Be Rechoreographed

Ever have the meeting after the meeting? The chitchat that can happen in the hallway, by the watercooler, and in the lunchroom disappear in the virtual world. Casual interaction between meetings and over a meal, a coffee, or a drink are where so many relationships build trust. Micro-interactions can often be where the foundation of or conclusion to decision-making happens. The nod, the breath sounds of agreement or frustration, and the informal "thank you" when the person passes you the Danish from across the table—these signals transform in 2D. But we still need the grunts, the eye contact, and the body language. We need to show we are human beings before we are job titles to build connections.

So, when spontaneous meeting doesn't happen, what happens to all of that quality interaction? It still lives in the margins between meetings and in the gestures that show you are paying attention. *The beginning of a meeting* is now where light and playful banter lies and trust is built. Most meetings will go too long to have the kind of conversation you would have had lingering between meetings. Too often, organizations run people through back-to-back-to-back videoconferences without even a bio break. Make the beginning of the meeting the time for people to show up a few minutes late. Pause if needed. Catch up on the dogs, cats, and kids that are nearby but not in the frame.

Use the breakout room function of many platforms to reengage in meetings. No one, not even the most focused individuals, can look at a screen hour after hour and not shut down. Instead of having a few people talking at the group or a fraction of the participants debating the whole time, use the breakout rooms to reengage every participant and then ask for summaries from one person in each room. Every person will thank you for the variation in form and the quality of ideas and debate will rise.

Use your chat platform or text messages to follow up after meetings. In the office, if someone says something really interesting, you say so as you leave the meeting and get a coffee. When someone is having a bad day, you ask if they are okay and natural next steps follow. Send a group chat or text if you want feedback that you normally would have gotten in the office kitchen. Send pointed texts to people to check on them or ask their opinion of what should happen next. Make sure not to leave people out. Every virtual communication lives forever and can, and will, be screenshot and forwarded.

Nonverbal Communication Evolves in 2D

The research, despite the myth that 93 percent of spoken words' meaning is nonverbal, cannot tell us how much nonverbal communication matters. What is certain? It matters a lot. Facial expressions, body language, and tone of voice are as critical in videoconferences as they are in the office. In a videoconference, you mostly only see from the chest up. Sometimes just a head. Often, poor lighting makes it hard to really see a person's facial expressions. And we don't know if the facial expression we see is a response to something we said or something off-screen.

Never forget, most people on a videoconference are constantly looking at themselves. When checking out your own facial expressions, keep yourself alert. The advice—smile—isn't quite right. See what you look like over time and make sure it reflects your true emotion and your expression isn't stuck. Do notice if you are frowning. Some people naturally frown when thinking. A frown, no matter how unintentional, throws off the energy in a meeting. Often, the balance between a half smile and an occasional head nod shows you are paying attention and listening for meaning.

When you really agree with a point, nod more vigorously. Give a thumbs-up. Use sign language that the team knows to show agreement. The same is true for disagreement. Don't just look grumpy. Putting your hand up in the virtual world may be necessary to gain attention of the leader or facilitator. Only use the emojis in the different platforms if it is accepted in your culture. When emojis are appropriate, there is no better feeling than giving a virtual presentation and seeing hundreds of cartoon hearts and thumbs-up fill the screen. Asking questions or saying thank you in the chat function, however, is always a way to engage the group and gather feedback.

Lastly, become extremely familiar with your tone and how it plays on the phone and on videoconference. When you sound annoyed, even if it is because just off the screen your partner or child is bothering you, it changes the meeting. You meant to make a simple point. Suddenly, because of the extra tone, your gentle critique becomes a vigorous counterpoint. The person hears you as harsh. And flat tone is just as dangerous. People will stop listening. Most people can't pay attention to all the faces on a videoconference with enough fluency to really read what's going on. They remember what they hear. What your tone portrays, they will never forget.

Cognitive Dissonance Raises Stress

Cognitive dissonance occurs when we hold two or more ideas in our heads at the same time and those ideas compete. When Leon Festinger first developed the theory in 1957, he was primarily interested in what happens to us when we experience mental inconsistency. What does it do to our stress levels? What happens to our behaviors? We want our expectation of the world and reality to match. When they don't, most people are motivated to either change their behavior to match the cognition, justify the cognition, or ignore the inconsistency. When communicating remotely, cognitive dissonance is real.

You want to present yourself professionally, but your business attire above the waist doesn't quite go with your sweatpants. You desperately want to impact a meeting of fellow executives, but just beyond the screen, your children are fighting. As you present before 500 people on a global webinar from your home office, above you your also-working-at-home partner yells at someone from your bedroom. Dogs and cats have no sense of when they should stay off camera. The necessity to overcome these distractions and communicate professionally is taxing. In some environments, family and felines are welcome. In others, they simply aren't.

Before virtual conversations, analyze what you need to be successful. You can't deny the dissonance if you want to communicate attentively. If you need quiet, negotiate it ahead of time. This matches the environment at home to the demands of the work. If an interaction is more casual, at the beginning, introduce your pets. This, in fact, starts a meeting off well. It lets people know you are human.

Sometimes you simply can't create an environment at home that matches the expectations of the office. Your manager simply may not understand your demands beyond the screen. If you are the leader or manager, have compassion for your team. Communicate in your one-to-ones about their work-from-home challenges and help them strategize what will make them great in the virtual world. If your manager is one of the less aware personalities who think home stress should not impact your work, you have a different cognitive dissonance problem to solve. If you can't get help from someone else in the organization, begin the search for an organization that matches your life.

We're All TV Stars Now: Framing, Lighting, and Sound

You are now both the TV director, gaffer doing lighting, and sound engineer of your own one-person show. You are the star, too. You do not need to be a technology genius to frame yourself well, have flattering lighting, and sound clear. You just need to prepare the setting. How people see and hear you in 2D impacts your ethos. Because ethos is relative, we can't tell you the exact way to present yourself. There are some moments when wearing a T-shirt at the meeting is perfect. Other times, formal attire is required. Match how you look to the formality of the audience's expectations just like you would pay attention to office attire.

Next, frame yourself intentionally. Usually, for a professional frame, make sure you are centered left and right, but not centered up and down. If you break the frame into thirds from top to bottom, your eyes should be in the upper third with space above your head. The camera itself should be placed just below eye level, presenting you at a slight angle. You may need to place your computer on books to get the right height for the camera. You should be far enough away from the lens so people can see you from around belly button up. This is called a medium shot and allows people to see your hands and arms. Sometimes you can't frame a medium shot. Make as much room as you can so people can see your gestures like they would in a face-to-face meeting.

Don't ignore what people see behind you, either. If you are creating a setting, make sure it is not too busy. Simple is always best. Remember that artifacts you include—books, art, furniture, and plants—tell a story. If you use a picture or scene as a virtual background, it can make people smile. It can also backfire and lower your ethos.

For lighting, we know you are not a television production crew. The principles behind lighting like a TV studio will still make you look better even if you are using the light next to your bed. Make sure you have enough light so that people can see your facial features. Avoid what are called hard shadows. You want people to look at you, not your shadow as you move. Instead of sitting directly under your recessed lighting in the kitchen, move back.

Professionals use what is called three-point lighting. The three lights are a key, a fill, and a backlight. The key light, the brightest, is either to the left or right of the camera. The fill light balances the key light's shadows on the other side of the camera. It should be a little less intense compared to the key light. The backlight is above and behind to create a subtle light around you and definition from the background. Understanding the principals can help you use what you have around the house. Usually, one light in front of you is enough, and lighting kits are inexpensive. Play with the light at different times of day to see what creates the best look.

For sound, the goal is to be heard clearly. Microphones use what are called pickup patterns. Most computers use omnidirectional patterns. They are designed to pick up everything in a room. Directional microphones pick up sound from a specific angle. Your wireless earbuds or headset might provide better sound than just your computer because you speak directly into a microphone that is aimed at your mouth. They are usually enough. A lavalier mic attached to your lapel, a directional mic plugged into your computer and just out of frame, or a headset will provide the best sound. Which mic should you use? A headset could make you look like a call center rep, and talking into a fancy mic like a radio host's might be more than you need. The answer depends on the quality of sound and the look demanded by the audience.

For every meeting on video, think about what you need for your ethos to be appropriate before the call. Schedule a videoconference with a colleague and test what you already have at home before creating a more technical, time-consuming setup. Once you have it figured out, you can spend all your time worrying about your message.

How a Virtual Meeting Platform Company Meets: LogMeIn

William Wagner is President and CEO at LogMeIn, the makers of GoToMeeting. In just seven years, the company has grown from 300 employees to 4,000 and sold at the end of 2019 for $4.3 billion. Three of the primary tools at LogMeIn are GoToMeeting, GoToWebinar, and GoToRooms. The primary mission for the GoTo brand, like many virtual platforms, is to eliminate friction in business communication. "Friction is the difficulty that arises in business communication when workers or companies and customers need to communicate remotely," Wagner told us.

The business community has seen a significant increase in the number of people working remote over the past 10 years. Beginning in 2020, even more people work virtually. "With the massive shift to work from home, meetings are no longer groups of people sitting far from the camera in a conference room" with a few people up on a screen. "Every meeting participant has their own square, their own camera and microphone. This makes for an easier time hearing and seeing meeting participants."

But how does LogMeIn, as a virtual platform company, do the virtual world better? Wagner says, "Even before COVID-19, we had developed a culture where the people at the office and in the conference room will each turn on their computers and cameras. It's for the benefit of the remote worker. This allows for a more neutral and comfortable communication experience." Normally, the person at home might feel less engaged. He can't see the facial expressions of all the people in the room. LogMeIn's simple adjustment levels the communication experience for every employee.

"It's important that people can come into a room and connect with technology as easily as using a phone." Even as a technology company, creating comfort with the tools is how you switch people from worrying about the "how" of interaction to the quality of conversations. Create training programs or at least samples of your communication platforms and tools. The less people have to think about method, the more they can focus on solutions.

"We also offset our visual live meetings with tools like Slack. Slack is a text-based tool with many threads to provide various topics of discussion. It allows email to be used for more formal communications. Slack might be for that informal banter that might normally happen before or after a meeting." Tools like Slack, group texting, and message boards are some ways to compensate for or even enhance the micro-interactions lost in the virtual world.

Choose the tools that work for your culture. LogMeIn is a culture of people who live and breathe technology. The tools have to be used so they become part of the culture. If they feel uncomfortable or even cumbersome, they won't produce impactful communication.

The Channel of Communication Matters

Channel of communication is an academic phrase that refers to the path messages take to be transmitted to receivers. For example, in a face-to-face meeting, the words are a channel, nonverbal cues are another channel, and slides a third channel. Onstage, the channel is the microphone and the sound system. Email is a written channel. On the telephone, the channel is the device transmitting your voice. The channel of communication matters in the virtual world because you want people listening to you to receive the message you intend. Imperfect or broken channels can change the intended message.

It's common for leaders to unconsciously use multiple channels, sometimes sending conflicting messages. For example, when giving feedback, you deliver the words your HR leader coached you to use. However, at the same time, another channel, your tone of voice, sends a conflicting message. Which message should the listener focus on? Which channel gets through? The skill is to be aware that these exist and to recognize that they behave differently in a remote experience.

When texting, tone is lost. On a phone line with a bad connection, you will repeat sentences or speak slower to create clarity. How many times have you had to redial someone when one or both of you had bad cell service? If the connection is too poor or the quality degrades too much, you reschedule the call. Many people feel that using video is just like being in person. This is not true if some people are in a place where they don't want you to see their background or their connection is bad so they keep their screens black.

The virtual world skews messages. For instance, you say something with a fun-loving sarcastic smile. The video quality doesn't capture the smile. The shadows from your poor lighting distract other participants so they miss part of your words. Now they think you are serious and there is a real problem when you were just trying to add humor to the moment. Managing and leading remotely requires awareness of various channels. The goal in picking the most effective channel is to reduce distraction from the intended message.

How to Create Equity in the Virtual World: Johns Hopkins University

Johns Hopkins University was ahead of its time in 2008 when Barbara Fivush, an award-winning pediatric clinician, planned and was chosen as the first director of the Office of Women in Science and Medicine. JHU was America's first research university, and of US academic institutions, it has largest research and development budget. In her role today as associate dean, Fivush supports thousands of women every year. Many schools have deans of faculty, who may have gender equality as a line item. It is the sole focus of Fivush's position.

Her leadership includes mentoring, coaching, seeking growth opportunities, and designing and implementing leadership development programs. The unique position has unique challenges, especially around helping leaders work from home successfully. Fivush told us, "It's my belief that working from home is much more difficult for women." The dissonance of parenting and professional life can impact virtual communication. "What's come out of the research is that women feel more burdened regarding childcare, meal preparation, and living space. So, they are thinking about that stuff while trying to work. The research does not demonstrate the same level of that with men."

To help with the dissonance, she creates programs that teach communication skills. "We want to empower women to do what they can, to promote themselves as executives and as leaders. We give them the tools to present that leadership quality." And quality communication in the virtual world begins with presence. "I tell people in my meetings that they must turn their video on. When the camera is not on, and all I see is their picture, it tells me they are not really committed to being at the meeting. I have no idea if they are listening or doing something else. Never keep your screen blank.

"At first, it was fun to put up a fake background, but don't do that. Clean up your room and show up. I don't want to talk to a photograph of you. If you want to be part of the meeting, you have to be a part of it. If it's a lecture, sure, black yourself out. But if you are in the meeting, be there and be as present as possible."

Because virtual meetings are not like being in the same room. "When in person, you see small side conversations, more specific things. But on videoconference, topics for discussion are more general. They are about the whole group. It's less intimate." And virtual meetings highlight how different tendencies can get in the way of effective communication. "There are those who like to talk and can comfortably interrupt at any time. But for people who don't like to talk, being virtual makes it much easier for them to sit back and accept that they will not participate. The whole muted, unmuted, be unmuted by the speaker, talk, don't talk: It's a much less natural flow of conversation. People less likely to speak are even less likely to speak."

So Fivush stresses the importance of intentional relationship building. "Once you stop developing the relationship with the people you work with, you lose a lot. We live in a social world, and context plays a huge part. If you never see people at all socially, they become just a name or face on the screen." In the virtual channels, building relationships takes intention. Relationship building virtually comes from curiosity. "Don't just ask a question because you want to make a sound. Ask meaningful questions. People need to learn how to do that."

Fivush emphasizes the move to more virtual communication has value, but it needs facilitation. "The upside is that I can bring teams together from different cities with ease. But moderators need to do their homework on how to get people engaged and feel a part of the meeting. I can't emphasize enough that you have to be there. You have to participate actively. Listen actively and join the conversation."

And remember that equity and virtual work includes gender as well as racial, geographical, and generational differences. People have different access to technology and space. People have different levels of awareness about each other's habits and cultures in different countries. Different individuals of all ages have different comfort levels with technology. Throw everyone into a virtual room and communication mistakes are inevitable. Pay attention to your team's differences, train everyone on technology and effective communication, and you can create arenas where everyone can start from the same place of comfort.

Facilitate or Fail

Facilitation skills are even more important in a remote setting. Great facilitators frame the purpose of a meeting at the beginning. In virtual gatherings, you have to reframe multiple times. Attention spans are smaller on-screen so begin every formal conversation with the purpose and remind people why the meeting matters at least one more time during the conversation. Remind them as well at the conclusion of the meeting.

Notice little changes to people's presence. Virtually, our peripheral nervous systems can no longer pick up on subtle changes in the room. In person, when someone lets out a gasp of air or people go deathly silent, a facilitator can generally appreciate the meaning of the differences. When change is noticed, it can be addressed. In an online format, when one person is talking, either other participants aren't visible or their faces can almost appear frozen. The facilitation skill is to scan the faces of participants while still listening to the speaker. Look for facial, posture, or eye movement changes. When something seems off, ask the person about it. It may be nothing. And truly engaging the virtual room means asking regularly what people are thinking and feeling.

Virtual facilitation also demands that everyone gets a chance to speak. Let people know the expectation for participation at the beginning of meetings so they aren't surprised. If you know people are shy or internal communicators, call on a few people at the same time rather than putting one person on the spot. Continue to invite participation because the casual conversations that used to happen around a meeting now have to be included in the meeting.

Leave enough time for questions. If more talkative participants have dominated or the content focused on a few people, make room for other people to offer their insight. You may have to ask about questions a few times. Quiet types need a few minutes to collect themselves, and everyone, when fatigued, may need a second cue to express their opinion.

Finally, the facilitator's final job in every meeting is to conclude who is doing what, and to ensure that all participants restate their commitments and that deadlines are clear. A clear set of takeaways is even more important in the virtual world because following up isn't as simple as poking your head in someone's office. Assign someone to send out notes, and list owners and deadlines next to completed agenda items.

Screen Fatigue, Breaks, and Isolation

When building a communication culture including virtual experiences, remember the impact of screen fatigue. Do you find yourself working from home and sitting in the same place for eight hours? It is a problem.

Screen fatigue is the feeling of lethargy that happens when someone sits in the same space, with the same posture, looking at the same screen for hours on end. Combine screen fatigue with cognitive dissonance, and clear messaging can be really difficult.

To manage screen fatigue, look away from your computer for a few seconds every 20 minutes. Studies have shown that this simple reset reinvigorates your focus. Stand up every 30 minutes. The study that looked at cognitive function and movement found people were smarter standing every 30 minutes and walking for a few minutes rather than only getting up after an hour or two. Schedule meetings so that participants can walk away from their computer at least every hour. Make 30-minute meetings 25 minutes and what might have been an hour, plan for 45 or 50 minutes. If you don't take these breaks, and if you don't plan them for your people as a leader, you prevent clear communication and hurt the performance of your team.

Even breaks, however, can't fix the emotional challenge that working remotely can be lonely at times. People can feel left out. The chitchat that happens around meetings doesn't include remote workers, and when everyone is remote, it is normal to feel isolated.

The communication mastery here falls on both sides. If you are the employee who is working remotely, include yourself by calling, messaging, or texting to stay present with your colleagues. Make an additional effort to compensate for the impromptu meetings and communication that is being missed through a virtual coffee or happy hour. If you are the manager, be sensitive to the members of your team who are not receiving those micro discussions that influence decisions and ideas. They need more than ever to see you notice that they need extra care. Paying attention to the emotional experience of the workers who are at home will build a culture where everyone knows they are valued.

The Future of Communication at Work Is a Hybrid

The world is resetting. Expectations about how we have to work are dissolving. At the same time, the forms of communication and tools available to every organization have expanded wildly. Every workplace can match the commercial, customer, and cultural needs of its people to communication methods that create clarity. The 2020 transformation of workplace culture allows every organization to ask a simple, powerful question: If I could start my business from scratch, how would I want people to communicate?

This begins with *framing*. What is your organization's business strategy? Whom are you selling to? What environment do you need to connect with people who want what you offer? Once you can answer the core business questions, you have the messages you want every employee to embrace. Now you can decide what methods and tools to use to spread the intelligence and gather your people. As we work globally, from offices and home, there are no more rigid conventions of how to work.

The tools and methods you use will be a *hybrid* of live and virtual communication. Where should people work from, home or the office? It's the wrong question. Instead ask what pattern allows different personalities to interact enough in person and virtually to innovate and produce while still having enough think time to do their work? Should meetings be in person or virtual? That is not the correct question either. Meetings should be looked at in terms of standing, seasonal, and emergency gatherings. Treat each gathering as its own chance to produce value. Many meetings will have live and virtual participants. The right question is which arena creates relationships where people build trust and love working together.

Sometimes everyone needs to be in the same room to feel each other's energy and ideas. Sometimes it is cheaper and more efficient to gather virtually. New technology will continue to develop that allows the answer to be both. Our new awareness about the tools and methods is now the instigation to reimagine what great messaging and interaction really looks like. What is ultimately certain is that creating a culture of communication needs to embrace the virtual world.

CHAPTER 14

COMMUNICATION AS A HARD SKILL

Creating a Culture of Communication

Does your organization have a strategy for communication? It most likely has a strategic direction based on segmentation, differentiation, and cost. It certainly has a marketing strategy that makes the public aware of what the organization offers that's unique. It probably has a talent management strategy to make sure that it has the right people performing at their highest levels. Your people also need to know your organization's communication strategy. How are you improving how they interact at work with global expectations of each person and each team in terms of effective communication?

A culture of communication is most easily created when the top executives and Board members are committed to the importance and value of an intentional, trust-building culture. In fact, that's the only way to ensure that impactful communication is supported, practiced, and measured. If people work hard on mastering the techniques and formats, but senior management shuts people down in meetings, it is almost impossible to push back.

That said, you can still go viral. Viral communication is about spreading the techniques and formats, live and virtually, one individual and one small group at a time. First, you have to do it. Wherever you work, the movement starts with you. Practicing the techniques and formats will increase your value to your organization and position you for career growth. You don't even have to describe what you're doing. Begin meetings with clear frames, give feedback based on the format, and motivate with intention. People will notice that you're doing something differently. People will ask if you've lost weight.

Then you want to find the people who are most excited about the topic. If someone thinks that communication is unimportant, you'll struggle to convince him. If he wants to commit only a few hours to learning how to communicate better, he isn't really ready to learn. If he is not curious about how to be more efficient and effective with the hours of his day, don't start with him.

You have people who are as fascinated by communication as they are by the discipline they were hired to deliver. These are the leaders, managers, and contributors whom you want to nurture and get on your team. They will gratefully spend extra time strengthening the way they do everything we've been talking about. Pour all your energy and resources into this group and the people around them because once they become better communicators, they will accelerate the adoption of the behaviors you want to see throughout your organization.

Your best training investment is in the people who want to learn.

You will still have the grumpy bears who think that paying attention to communication is not using time wisely. Watch them closely because they can be a powerful measurement of whether your culture is changing. When they start speaking differently, running meetings like your early adopters, or adding color to presentations that you've never seen from them before, the change is happening.

Even then, there will still be the malcontents who think that intentionally working on communication is stupid. They will actually say, "This is stupid. I have work to do." You, as a leader, have to make a choice here. These people are either a helpful opportunity for everyone else to hone their skills—just as a disruptive technology spurs innovation, or they need to find a new culture where their style works. Every time you help someone move on well, your power as an effective leader and manager increases.

Becoming a master communicator comes from learning the techniques and formats, practicing them regularly, and partnering with people who can help you improve. The best organizations take communication seriously. They train regularly with real problems as case studies. Whether your culture is there today or you are the first to start the movement, you can be a driver of an intentional plan for improving communication.

How to Become a Better Communicator: Google

On Google's corporate website, there is a list of the "Ten things Google has found to be true." It's a list of one-paragraph reflections stating what the organization believes, and the ninth describes the communication culture that the firm has created:

9. You can be serious without a suit.

Google's founders have often stated that the company is not serious about anything but search. They built a company around the idea that work should be challenging and the challenge should be fun. To that end, Google's culture is unlike any in corporate America, and it's not because of the ubiquitous lava lamps and large rubber balls, or the fact that the company's first chef used to cook for the Grateful Dead. In the same way Google puts users first when it comes to our online service, Google Inc. puts employees first when it comes to daily life in our Googleplex headquarters. There is an emphasis on team achievements and pride in individual accomplishments that contribute to the company's overall success. Ideas are traded, tested and put into practice with an alacrity that can be dizzying. Meetings that would take hours elsewhere are frequently little more than a conversation in line for lunch and few walls separate those who write the code from those who write the checks. This highly communicative environment fosters a productivity and camaraderie fueled by the realization that millions of people rely on Google results. Give the proper tools to a group of people who like to make a difference, and they will.

Begun in 1998, the company reached 200 employees by 2001, and by 2020 more than 120,000 Googlers staff its 70 offices and thousands of virtual home offices around the world.

Google consistently ranks at the height of places people want to work. The reason: the entire company seeks to foster the philosophy of the original culture. In his role as head of people operations, Laszlo Bock helped maintain the behaviors that have made Google the model of an effective communication culture. Bock told us:

> As you get bigger, you inevitably become a bit more anonymous, as you can no longer know everyone personally. The tone and nature of communication therefore changes. You need to work harder to make it explicit that the culture and communication matter.
>
> Every chance I got, I talked about how important communication is. Whether it was at our weekly company all-hands meeting called TGIF, where anyone can ask senior management questions, or at one of our People Operations quarterly meetings, or by sending emails, it's important to emphasize that communication is important. It doesn't matter what you're doing if you don't communicate it well.

As a leader, Bock, currently cofounder and CEO of Humu, became the biggest cheerleader when people were doing it right. He said that "outside my office, I had what I call my 'wall of happy.' When someone in People Operations received a positive note from an internal customer, we posted it online and on the wall of happy. When the notes were about communication, I broadcasted them so that people could see not just that communication matters, but that it matters to me as a leader in the organization."

It is best when great communication starts at the top, but it doesn't have to, and this is why improving communication can be viral. "You don't need every leader saying it, but you need a minimum critical mass," Bock said. "And a 'leader' is not just an executive. It is anyone who has a voice that is listened to, anyone who is viewed as an authority on the culture." But the top leadership at Google does model effective communication, and that instantly gives every teammate permission to value it as part of her professional development.

Executives like Bock have a humility in their vision of how to communicate that belies their sensational success and, in fact, creates a culture that continues to inspire innovation and growth. It's how they work with their teams every day. "The most important thing [about modeling great communication], in my experience, has been demonstrating vulnerability," explained Bock. "The models where I've seen it most successfully done are where leaders at every level of the company can say, 'I was wrong, I made a mistake,' and where there's no shame attached to that admission. In fact, there should be a little bit of nobility in it."

Vulnerability doesn't work in every culture. In some cultures, in fact, showing that you are weak might get you fired. But that's because the culture is broken. The freedom for a leader to be vulnerable, to talk openly about his mistakes, is another metric of a healthy communication culture. "That vulnerability makes it okay for everybody else to have the same vulnerability, so you get more interesting ideas, more creativity, and a lot more learning," observed Bock. "Chris Argyris wrote about single- and double-loop learning, and how for bright, accomplished people, their ability to learn from failure sometimes shuts down when they fail. Giving people permission to fail reactivates their ability to learn."

At Google, learning is paramount, and when it comes to communication, the company understands that you can't force that learning. Bock said that "What I've observed is that people have different moments of readiness to learn about different things. Teaching communication and how to do it effectively requires that you identify those moments and then teach in ways that are adaptive to certain individuals." You can teach people to communicate more effectively, but it's much easier to do that when they are ready and in the way that is best customized for how they learn.

Warning: What you are about to read is going to blow your mind. This is the model. This is what you want your company to have available, so that when people are ready to learn about how to be better leaders, managers, and teammates, they can.

Google is the master of formal communication training, the informal expectations it sets for every employee, and employing patterns of communication every day that don't waste time. Bock shared:

> On the formal training side, if you imagine a box, and in the middle of the box is everything it takes to be a phenomenal communicator, every

person will want to access that box from a different face—each face is a different learning process, style, or teachable experience, so we tried to create situations where based on whatever you need as a person, whatever will teach you best, you have access to it.

So Google has one-on-one coaching, courses on communication where that is the focus, and courses like the Advanced Leadership Lab, where a component is how you are perceived and how you manage those perceptions, but that's embedded in a broader learning curriculum. Google has some people who just teach various topics on their own. Google also has informal networks about how you can become a better communicator and speaker—there are lots of different ways to get to that same core content and learning.

Less formally, the company also believes a number of things to be true, and this is deeply embedded in the DNA of the culture. Everything is data-driven. So you can't go to a meeting and assert, "Well, I think product X isn't very good." You need to have detailed data to support your opinion. The culture says, "Number one, don't make a statement unless you can back it up, and number two, make all the data transparent." If a project is going poorly, you report that it is going poorly, and you say, "Here's what we're doing." Then you have a constructive conversation focused on problem solving rather than finger-pointing.

Three, Google very much has a discussion model, a debate model that is a dialectic. In almost every meeting, you have thesis and antithesis, and you come to synthesis. If you watch anyone who has been here for a long time, he will invariably set up a discussion where somebody takes one position and then someone else, for the sake of argument, takes the extreme opposite position because the belief is that you will get to a better answer if you start discussions from very different perspectives rather than having everybody 80 percent aligned.

This massively influences the nature of communication because suddenly it's okay to have wacky ideas; it's okay to push the envelope; it's okay to yell and shout and disagree—*with the idea*. As a result of this, you have a process where you air a lot of views, and people who aren't even directly involved in the process trust that all the views were heard because they know how this kind of discussion happens here, and they can trust that process.

The immediate criticism from any other organization is obvious: "We're not Google. How can we possibly create this kind of culture, because this sort of environment doesn't just happen on its own?" True. An effective communication culture takes a strategic focus on deciding how you will communicate, but it doesn't take Google's resources. The dialectical method of meeting and the transparent, collaborative process of working together were the foundation of Google's culture before the company's epic rise.

Bock has seen the same thing across different kinds of businesses, too:

I was on a panel with Jack DePeters, SVP and COO of Wegmans Food Markets, Inc. It's a supermarket chain, in an industry with very narrow margins in general, and it was picked as the best company to work for in the United States and has been near the top of the list ever since. As we talked, I realized that Wegmans had far more in common with Google than even most other companies in our industry did because Wegmans thought about its employees as people, trusted them, and gave them autonomy. It trained them, coached them, and rewarded them.

I think there is a huge opportunity. Workers are looking for something different from what they looked for 20 to 30 years ago, and that comes back to what you believe about people and what kind of environment you create. I think a lot of what we do here, the underlying principles, can be done in a lot of places if people want to risk it.

Strangely, the biggest risk for most leaders is saying what they actually think about people. Communicating your raw beliefs about how people do their best work is dangerous because people won't agree with you, and focusing on skills like communication has been considered "soft" for decades. But when you focus on communication and when you do it with the intention of strengthening the culture, the resulting conversation and inevitable debate produce core principles that fuel behavior.

Bock said he was excited about coming to work every day because of what was possible at Google. The opportunities would have been stunted without the firm's explicitly stated core beliefs: "The most compelling part for me was the belief at Google that people are fundamentally good. If you give people freedom, they will amaze you." Valuing people rather than controlling them is so simple. It is essential to creating a communication culture in which people aren't afraid to say what they really think, challenge the norms of your work, and, from that free exchange of ideas, innovate.

How to Develop Effective Communicators: Harvard Business School

As Google's varied methodologies for teaching communication demonstrate, people learn to master communication in different ways. You have to decide the methodology and style of content that you, your team, and, if you're the leader, your organization will employ to help people improve. Your culture is unique. The different ways Harvard Business School (HBS) teaches its leaders in its programs reveal the spectrum of methodologies that foster communication skill.

In most classes for the 900 master of business administration students at HBS, half of the grade is based on class participation. Part of the admission process is an interview in which every applicant is vetted. In the same way that Google uses biodata to pick the right people, Harvard uses interviews to determine whether students have the communication potential and the confidence to succeed in a rigorous environment with some of the smartest people in the world.

At Harvard Business School, there are no classes and no professor specializing in communication. This is a relatively new approach. Tony Mayo, who directed the school's leadership initiative for almost two decades, told us that "When I went to the MBA program 30 years ago, communication was part of the curriculum. It was taught through communication specialists, videotaping, and learning specific skills. Over the years, HBS has moved away from a required course on communication."

But that doesn't mean that HBS doesn't teach communication. In fact, because of the explicit expectation that class participation is graded, every class becomes an exercise in improving the way students listen and speak. Students don't learn from abstract theory in textbooks; rather, they use the case method model. Each class discusses and debates real-world examples of the principles being learned, which forces students to formulate their ideas out loud in front of peers who will happily challenge them if they disagree. Explains Mayo:

> We focus on situational leadership, knowing how to employ different leadership styles for different situations and knowing the right questions to ask—all of which are communication dependent. The thought in the MBA program is that if you put yourself in the case protagonist role and a significant portion of your grade is based on class participation, you are forced to learn how to communicate. To be successful, you need to listen effectively to the discussion to ensure that your follow-up comments are relevant and move the conversation forward.

What Harvard does with its MBA class is the first of two extremes on the spectrum of how to teach communication: make it an expectation of your culture. The strategy is Darwinian and reveals talent quickly. If you demand a certain kind of behavior from the members of your team, just as Google expects every employee to make every opinion data driven and to have that data be transparent, they know what's expected from them. The expectations for class participation at HBS are outlined, and students receive feedback on their performance. In every class, the top 15 to 20 percent get 1s, the middle 70 to 75 percent get 2s, and the bottom 10 percent get 3s. Enough 3s and you could receive an academic warning. The other side of Darwin is that not everyone can rise. This method immediately reveals who needs extra help—or who isn't fit for your culture. There is a bottom level of performers, even at Harvard, and that's where coaching comes in.

Students who need help can get personal coaching, but notice that this doesn't happen first. The program doesn't start with a course on communication that gives everyone the chance to develop skills. *In every organization, the choice in teaching effective communication is where you begin.* Do you train people right away in the kind of communication you want to be their normal pattern of behavior, or do you introduce them into the environment, expect them to learn, and provide help when they need it?

The methodology at the other end of the spectrum, intentional training, is also used at Harvard in courses offered by the Leadership Initiative. HBS created the Leadership Initiative in 2000 to champion research on leadership that could apply directly to its mission to train students who could make a difference in the world. The Leadership Initiative offers 10 weeks each year of rigorous training for leaders in organizations: weeklong intensives on leadership best practices, custom leadership programs for corporations, and leadership development programs for high potentials (executives with 10 to 15 years' experience who have been identified by companies as their future top leadership).

The communication module in these courses began in 2003 in building the high potentials agenda. "We talked to 60 companies around the world," says Mayo, "and we asked them, 'What do your emerging leaders need?' One of the core competencies we heard was communication: both writing and speaking, effectively and concisely, including strategic positioning statements." Plain and simple, leaders need help with their elevator pitch. This sounds absurd, but having talent in finance or even communication-driven disciplines like marketing or sales doesn't instantly mean that you can communicate effectively and with brevity.

As a result, out of the four-and-a-half-day intensive program, a full day is spent on communication. Mayo notes:

> These are executives who are on the fast track, and the program is all about personal leadership: how to manage teams, lead change, manage performance, be an inspirational leader, and communicate. We focus on how you better understand your leadership style and what works or doesn't work for you. The communication module is about taking people out of their comfort zone and providing them with a potentially new set of personal tools.

The day of communication programming focuses on the leader's presence and how to bring more vulnerability to presentations. As Mayo reflects, "The real nugget is around incorporating storytelling into business presentations, telling more about yourself to connect more to your audience." As Bock emphasized at Google, vulnerability is one of the core traits of effective communicators, and Harvard teaches it through communication exercises.

In the executive education programs, the group of 100 is broken down into seven- or eight-person teams. They run improvisational drills like telling your personal story in eight sentences, then six, then four, and finally two. The exercise is basic, but the ability to do it well takes practice. This kind of exercise in front of talented strangers, perhaps even competitors in your field, sticks with the participants. Mayo mentions that:

> There is a huge uptick in the latter part of the week in terms of participation, and we see a wide range of emotions as people stretch outside their comfort zones. The vast majority of people who go through the training feel that it improves their communication style. It's one of the concrete things you can walk away and do fundamentally differently when you get back to work.

But even in the executive programs, notice the subtle difference between Harvard and Google. Says Mayo: "When we have a case protagonist [someone who is solving a case study in front of the group], we'll unpack her leadership style and talk about the kind of connections, but not about, 'Here's how you respond to them.' We talk about how to be persuasive and about communication as a tool, but the nuts and bolts are in the workshop." The executive program's way of teaching leaders reveals a second set of choices when developing effective communicators: the content you use to train can range from entirely situational training to purely theoretical, skill-based learning.

In addition to the situational learning that happens when any leader or manager helps her teammates break down how to solve a problem better, Google offers classes. Google teaches employees—when they are ready—the theory and practice of *how* to communicate more effectively. Harvard doesn't. Harvard Business School chooses, even in its training sessions, to drive behavior by putting leaders in a situation in which they need to communicate effectively so that they can figure out their leadership style. MBA students would have to go to a different school in the university if they wanted a class that taught them how to be a better public speaker.

The two choices for your culture, whether you're bringing a new teammate on board or planning the communication training for 100,000, are: What method will help your people learn? If you choose to train them, what style of content will produce effective communicators?

Harvard Business School's MBA program is the farthest on the spectrum toward the setting of expectations as the method to teach communication. Maytag sales training, for instance, is at the other extreme, where you spend months learning how to sell without ever looking at a washing machine. Since HBS is an academic environment, expectations work there. This method won't work in every culture. If one of your teammates is afraid of public speaking and you push her too hard too quickly, she may not recover.

Most likely, your organization will fall somewhere in the middle. Bain Consulting, for instance, trains everyone on the Bain Voice when that person joins the company. After onboarding, using the method becomes an expectation that is part of each consultant's review process. Suria KLCC in Southeast Asia trains its senior managers in situational and theoretical communication first so that they can model effective communication and then become the teachers for the rest of the organization.

The key is to have a strategy concerning how you will help your people make communication a priority in how they work. The strategy should be custom designed to fit the needs of your culture, based on the current state of your organization today and what you'd like it to be. Now that you know the options, the only wrong method is not to have a strategy to help your people learn.

How to Improve Communication in Your Organization: The White House

Taking a strategic approach to helping others communicate effectively is as present in the most pressure-infused office in the world—the White House—as it is at Google and Harvard. Doris Kearns Goodwin worked for the White House as a fellow after completing her doctoral work at Harvard. She became Lyndon Baines Johnson's personal confidante during his last year in office and helped him complete his memoirs during the last years of his life. As a presidential expert who taught at Harvard, Pulitzer Prize–winning author of five books on the lives of presidents, and TV commentator, her reflections about the environment during Johnson's White House reveal what kind of communication is essential in a workplace that literally changes the world every day:

> What's interesting is that when you think about the communication channels that LBJ set up to the Congress, everybody in that White House knew that that was the utmost priority for him: to have good relationships with the Congress, to know exactly where the bills that he needed to have passed were. He had these big maps in his office to let him know where each bill was in a committee, what stage it was at, and what it needed to happen for it to be reported to the next stage, and then he would start to call the individual congressmen who could be obstacles at that stage, make sure that they understood how important the bill was for him, and promise them whatever he needed to in order to get it through.

Imagine it. In your business, on one large wall, you have a map of where all the most important communication is happening, what initiatives are being discussed, and what obstacles need to be overcome to reach your goals. It is natural to do this with supply chains, sales leads, and organizational charts, but not with communication. Imagine Lyndon Johnson scribbling on this map to make sure he knew whom he had to talk to in order to get the result he wanted. What if you prepared for every conversation with that kind of intensity? Goodwin relates how:

> All of the people within the White House knew that Johnson's congressional relationships were important to him and therefore to them, so they would be ferreting out information that he needed in order to know where these various bills were at any particular moment in time. And then he would call the various congressmen for breakfast, he'd invite them for lunch, or he'd have them for cocktails. He would call them in the middle of the morning if he needed to.

There's that famous story of him calling a senator at 2 a.m. and saying, "I hope I didn't wake you up," and the senator saying, "Oh, no, I was just lying here, hoping my president would call." He once said that you had to court the congressmen even more ardently than you would court your wife, or the most beautiful woman.

Once a bill was passed, he would invite the congressmen and senators who had been helpful in getting it through to the signing ceremony. And he would make sure to have the local newspapers from those people's districts and states there, and then he would then tell them how great these people were, that these people were the heroes who got the bill through, so that the news would make it back to their local district or state.

Of course, you're not the president of the United States. Your people are not sitting on their beds waiting for your email on their smartphone. Oh, wait. Yes, they are. Even if you're not the executive of a big company, numerous devices connect your people every moment of every day. High performers wait for the next piece of news from work about what you are doing and what needs to get done. They are ready to be just as attentive as that senator who perked up for the president in the middle of the night.

But that doesn't mean that the communication is working. Effective communication does not happen naturally. You have to be as intense as LBJ, as focused on learning as Harvard, and as ready to help people learn as Google. You have to come up with your answers about what resources you are going to provide, how to challenge people to use them, and how to measure progress the way you keep track of success.

How Your Organization Can Master Communication

Leaders in every generation have faced pressure like Atlas holding up the world. But the best of them, like Aristotle changing the way we think forever and Lincoln using humor to rebuild a nation, never stopped focusing on the power that communication could bring to every relationship and every action. You can be the best. Stress won't go away, but if you make strategic communication a priority, a behavior that you demand from yourself and your team, you can recover from stress faster and use pressure to build stronger relationships. You can produce more innovative, creative results.

Instead of an issue lingering—whether it's a product problem that won't go away or a strategy decision that keeps being repeated because people are afraid to make the hard choice—you have the techniques and formats to wake people up. If you are training everyone to lead, people will be able to manage more effectively because they will notice that things aren't going well. They will refuse to waste a moment. They will take advantage of casual moments like lunch to build relationships that are deeper than work, and then turn those personal connections into the opportunity to be honest about what they do every day. And like LBJ and his map on the wall, your people will measure and track communication the way they do the capital on hand to run your business.

Here are the steps to build teammates and a culture that masters communication. The order is not important, but the categories are essential.

1. *Decide what you believe.*

- Where is communication a strategic priority in your work and your organization?
- Do you want to set expectations for behavior, as Harvard does for its MBAs, and offer communication coaching for those who need it, or do you want to train it, deciding between situational and skill-based learning, as Harvard does in its executive learning programs? Will you do both?
- What needs to be measured to prove that your teams are communicating effectively?

Answer these questions, and you can begin building a system that works for your culture.

2. *Develop your communication strategy.* Find the low-hanging fruit. There is something that you can do today to cut

expenses, and there is definitely something that you can do today to improve communication.

- EMI started holding weekly lunches.
- Kadient Software added an all-company meeting.
- Harvard added improvisation exercises to its leadership programs.

An assessment of your current culture will reveal what your needs are. The method is simple: have one person interview 20 people and ask, "What three things will improve our communication?" Leave the question general and see what similar answers emerge. Make sure the person asking the questions has the ethos to get honest feedback. Hire a communication specialist if you need to, because an outsider's perspective will help you craft experiences that resonate. The responses won't be complicated, and then you can create a strategy that will virally change the behaviors. Find the way in which you can be different and impactful.

- Bain Consulting follows a deductive, answer first format when talking to clients.
- Google holds dialectical meetings.
- Aristotle traced the human behaviors that persuade people.

The secret is to pay attention. Trust comes from the way you communicate, and everyone needs help in knowing how to pay attention to the needs of his teams and his clients. Create an environment in which people know the way you want communication to matter, and it will affect everything you do.

3. ***Create a box of resources.*** Ameriprise Financial has webinars, podcasts, e-learning, and white papers, so that its advisors know how to connect with clients. Google has courses on every kind of communication subject, situational and skill-based, delivered via every conceivable platform. If you want your people to improve, at least offer a shelf of books about great communication and leadership, a simple list of

website links, or a blog where everyone in the company offers her favorite resource on how the best leaders and managers communicate.

4. *Create an arena map.* If people know where to go with their issues about what you do at work, they will stop spinning. Every employee needs one-on-one time with a leader. With just a regular hour once a week, every working group can usually solve important problems. Get the company together once a quarter to share vision and ask pressing questions. If your leaders validate everyone who has the guts to participate, trust and energy will soar. If everyone knows when the meetings concerning the major initiatives that affect everyone happen, people can show up and have an impact. Better yet, leaders can direct them to the meetings where their creativity can inspire others.

5. *Measure communication.* Generate straightforward questions. These are based on the observable signs of leaders and managers who use the six techniques. Create a scorecard and measure the development of communication in your team of a few or organization of thousands. For instance:

Have everyone answer these questions on the following scale: 1—Always, 2—Sometimes, or 3—Never.

1. Do you feel calm throughout the workday?
2. Are you getting the reactions you expect when you present at or contribute to meetings?
3. Are you meeting your deadlines?
4. Do you intentionally frame every conversation and communication?
5. Do you feel valued for your work?
6. Do you know how to speak in order to have impact on your listeners?

Have people fill out the scorecard each month. Not only are you emphasizing the importance of communication, but the closer you get to 1 as an average, the more improvement you will see in individuals and in your culture.

Another way to measure communication is to test people every month on some aspect of the speaking they have to do every day. Whether it's describing what makes your organization unique, making a sales presentation, or just their ability to frame a meeting, make them show off. Score it on a scale of 1 to 3 the way Harvard Business School grades class participation. The people getting the 3s consistently may not be the right fit. They need to know that they are underperforming so that they can either improve with coaching or find a workplace where they can succeed.

Communication Is a Hard Skill

Creating a culture of communication isn't a gimmick or a fad for performance improvement. When communication is emphasized, you get Google. People are motivated and love their jobs, they anticipate problems, and brainstorming produces high-quality innovations. Without effective communication, organizations shut down. You know that effective communication is missing when the environment is highly political, people talk about one another instead of to one another, and work just isn't fun. Unhealthy communication environments can only attract top talent with money. Employees aren't engaged, and you risk the future success of the organization.

Creating a culture of communication means creating an environment that sees stellar communication as essential, considers the development of it to be part of the norms of daily work, and rewards people for it. Too many leaders, managers, and teammates feel that if someone has to practice conversations, he's not good at what he does. In a culture of communication, it's a good thing to practice. You can go to your boss and say, "Will you practice with me?" Intentional communication is fostered, is seen as a strength, and is the goal for everyone in the organization.

If you don't have this kind of culture where you work, be the first to change the way you work. You can learn what Aristotle taught more than 2,000 years ago and leaders throughout history in every kind of organization have practiced every day. Master the techniques. Master the formats. Build an intentional communication culture for the future. Make communicating effectively a daily priority in your life, and you can master communication at work.

INDEX

ABOUT THE AUTHORS

Dr. Ethan F. Becker is a second-generation speech coach/trainer and president at the Speech Improvement Company, the oldest communication coaching and training firm in the United States. He specializes in motivating teams, strengthening executive communication, controlling fear of speaking, and developing effectiveness in public presentations. He has worked with Apple, IBM, Bain Capital, Sony ATV, Canon, Boston Scientific, the New York Giants, the FBI, Harvard University, Johns Hopkins University, Boston College, and clients all over the world.

Jon Wortmann is an executive coach, trainer, and speaker on leadership, communication, and resilience. Trained at Harvard University, he has delivered more than 3,000 live and virtual presentations globally. Jon is the author of five books and is an NCAA and PGA Tour golf coach.